HISTORY IN CAMERA

SEASIDE FASHIONS 1860-1939

A study of clothes worn in or beside the sea

Avril La

Shire Publications Ltd

Printed in Great Britain by C. I. Thomas & Sons (Haverfordwest) Ltd, Press Buildings, Merlins Bridge, Haverfordwest, Dyfed SA61 1XF.

British Library Cataloguing in Publication Data: Lansdell, Avril. Seaside Fashions 1860-1939: a study of clothes worn in or beside the sea. — (History in Camera; no. 10). 1. British costume, history. I. Title. II Series. 391.00941. ISBN 0-7478-0066-9.

Front cover: *Holiday fun in 1908. The girl on the left wears all-in-one bathing combinations with sailor collar and wide sash; the woman on the right wears an older-fashioned bathing-dress with a knee-length skirt and frilled drawers.*

Title page: *Three-year-old Dorothy Wood is pictured in 1902 ready for the beach in a short pleated skirt topped with a knitted jumper and bonnet.*

Opposite: *Mr and Mrs Smith at Palm Bay about 1927 — a middle-aged couple relaxing in deck-chairs.*

Contents

Above: *Bathing-costumes and a magnificent Japanese parasol of 1910. The girl in the striped bathing-dress wears a belted tunic, drawers and a mob-cap. The younger girl wears a 'combination' costume, made in one piece with a gathered neckline. Although it cannot be seen, this costume, too, probably has a belt round the waist.*

1. Introduction: the British seaside

Before 1700 the sea was to most British people a barrier, the defence of their island, a source of food, a highway to other lands, a battleground or a graveyard. The sea was feared or exploited and the beach was no more than its edge. Those who used the beach did so for the purpose of gathering food or getting into boats. It was not until the early eighteenth century that the idea of using the sea and beach for any other purpose began to seem even reasonable. At first it was not for pleasure. Sea-bathing, as recommended by the doctors of the time, was carried out in winter and usually at an early hour of the morning. It was an extension of the principle that water, enriched with minerals, can bestow good health. This had been known from Roman times but the waters used had been those of inland springs. The movement towards the sea was to bring the decline of the elegant inland spas, such as Bath and Tunbridge Wells, whose fashionable delights had been only for the rich and privileged, and the growth of seaside towns such as Blackpool, Ramsgate and Scarborough, where all tastes and social classes could be entertained.

The first 'seaside town' was already a spa. This was Scarborough in North Yorkshire. Like all spas it had a Master of Ceremonies whose job was to organise the use of the facilities and the entertainments offered alongside them. In the 1730s Scarborough's Master of Ceremonies was Richard (Dicky) Dickenson, a short man famous for his wit. He was quick to recognise that the doctors' recommendation of sea-bathing could extend the fashionable season at Scarborough and be an additional source of interest and revenue to the town. Visitors, therefore, paid for the privilege of using the beach.

After the early-morning dip — nobody stayed in long — the pleasures of the town were there to be enjoyed. These included assembly rooms for cards and gossip, a lending library, restaurants and facilities for walking and riding as well as the opportunity to drink the mineral waters for which Scarborough had originally been famous. Nobody lingered on the beach; clothes for riding, promenading and dancing were those considered important.

Bathing continued to be a medically recommended cure-all throughout the eighteenth century and seaside villages all round England, Scotland and Wales began to cater for a new influx of middle-class visitors in search of health. The bathing-machine was invented at Margate by Benjamin Beale, a Quaker, in 1753,

1 (left). *Early bathing-machines with folding canopies, as depicted in a fashion print of 1814. (See also plate 10.)*

2 (right). *A printed licence for a bathing-machine at Worthing in the 1850s.*

to enable women to bathe in modest seclusion. It was a hut on wheels with a door and steps to reach it. The user entered from the rear and undressed while a horse pulled it down the beach and into the sea until the floor was just above the waves. When the horse stopped a canopy was let down over the door and steps, and the bather could emerge and descend into the water hidden from vulgar gaze by the canopy; she was then led into the sea by a female 'dipper', the forerunner of the Victorian bathing women beach attendants.

By the end of the eighteenth century the seaside had gained royal approval. George III took his first dip, from a bathing-machine, at Weymouth in 1789. His son, the Prince of Wales, had already enjoyed visits to Brighthelmstone (later to become Brighton) and by 1787 had built his first modest Pavilion there. The pleasures of the seaside were gradually taking over from the idea of a cold early-morning winter dip for health. The early nineteenth-century writers stressed the benefit of sea-air, in summer, for both health and enjoyment. The enjoyment for the young men, particularly at Brighton, included watching the female bathers (through telescopes), for Brighton bathing-

3. *An 1860s seaside photograph, one of a stereoscopic pair, of Arched Rock, Freshwater Bay, Isle of Wight. The five figures are of middle-class holidaymakers who are exploring the rocks and collecting shells and seaweed, a popular mid-Victorian holiday pastime. A photographer's tripod and camera are almost hidden behind the rock wall on the left but are visible as a reflection in the rock pool. Photography was also a middle-class hobby in spite of the cumbersome equipment needed.*

machines never had hoods. The seaside resorts had one advantage over the long-established inland spas, where everything was highly organised and controlled. From the beginning there was an undertone of sexual freedom associated with the seaside; people undressed on the beach; men bathed naked; telescopes could be used by young women as well as young men. The visitors were on holiday and this contributed to a sense of release from everyday social restrictions. In the words of a later, Victorian, music-hall song, 'You can do all sorts of things at the seaside that you cannot do at home'.

The railways played a great part in this, making hitherto inaccessible places in Wales, Devon and the south and east coasts into popular holiday towns. The Bank Holiday Act of 1871 gave all working-class people at least four statutory days holiday a year. The most popular of these was the August Bank Holiday and many families would make this their day out at the seaside. For the poorest of them it was their only holiday of the year and they were determined to make the most of it. Ideally it was as lively, as gregarious and as entertaining as possible.

Entertainment, in many forms, was part of most Victorian seaside holidays. As visitors began to linger on the beach, so musicians and street sellers came to join them. There were brass bands, highland pipers, barrel-organs, Punch and Judy shows, dancing dogs, tumblers, blacked-up minstrels (an idea imported

4. Anstey's Cove, Torquay, in 1884. These bathing-machines are attached to winches which control their position on the beach. They have no canopies but, being in a secluded quiet bay, may never have had them.

from the United States), vendors of all kinds of food, drink, souvenirs and seaside accessories — hats, parasols, buckets and spades, shrimping nets — together with photographers and artists, guaranteeing a likeness in a tintype photograph or a charcoal sketch, all announcing themselves or crying their wares at the tops of their voices.

The popular resorts became crowded, noisy and uninhibited. At the water's edge the bathing-machines reigned supreme; on some beaches they were no longer drawn into the sea by horses but were hauled up and down the beach by winches or by teams of men, moving them with the tide. In this case they faced out to sea, and a plank was laid from the beach across the edge of the water. The would-be bather went in at the land side, undressed and descended the steps on the seaward side. The canopies disappeared; bathing was a pleasure to be enjoyed, preferably on a warm sunny day, the most popular times being between 11 o'clock and 12.30 in the morning and 3 o'clock and 4.30 in the afternoon. Even so, men and women bathed at different times or on different parts of the beach, and bathing-machines were strictly controlled and licensed. Swimming lessons were available, the dippers of Regency days turning into beach attendants and swimming teachers. Bathing became an activity also enjoyed, or endured, by children, who added to it an activity unthought of in the eighteenth century, that of paddling in the edge of the water.

Paddling did not require the removal of all one's clothes. So long as the legs were bare and the rest of the clothing was held

5. *Girls paddling at Blackpool, about 1897. Two of the girls are wearing capes with big collars; the oldest has a straw hat as well. The child without a coat is wearing an overall with a yoke over her dress, which has long sleeves and a big collar. The girls are all wearing knee-length drawers. This picture is from a stereoscopic pair.*

6. *An Edwardian holidaymaker, in white flannels, blazer and boater hat, relaxes with a pipe in a tent above the beach near Dawlish, Devon, about 1906. Camping holidays were in vogue in Edwardian days and ready-pitched tents could be hired for a night or a week or more. This tent is obviously on such a camp site and the young man may well have been on a cycling tour of the south coast, a popular type of holiday for the energetic. There is a bicycle just behind the tent.*

7. *A beach hut at Burbary, Devon, in the late 1930s. The huts were small, not much larger than the old bathing-machines, but they were stationed at the top of the beach and could be used for changing into bathing-costumes, for storing deck-chairs and towels, and for tea-making equipment. Families would hire a beach hut by the week and, by using it as their day-time base, needed to take only bed and breakfast accommodation for their holiday. There were usually bylaws which prohibited people sleeping in them. This family picture shows a selection of the clothes worn to the beach by a group of middle-class suburban holidaymakers about 1937 or 1938. Note the ruched cotton bathing-costume worn by the woman on the right. The ruching was achieved by the use of shirring elastic, a fashion that was to continue into the 1940s and 1950s for bright-coloured swimming costumes for women and small children.*

clear of the sea the shallow water could be enjoyed. By the end of
the nineteenth century paddling had developed into the highlight
of a visit to the seaside, even for adults, and especially for the day
trippers for whom swimming could be too expensive (bathing-
machines and costumes had to be hired) or take too long. Paddling was free; it could be done as a family and enjoyed at the edge
of a crowded beach, noisy with entertainers.

The Victorian style of seaside holiday continued into the
twentieth century with few changes. There were both quiet and
lively seaside places. The quiet and genteel resorts gained a few
amenities; the more vulgar places calmed down a little. Minstrels
gave way to pierrots and mixed bathing became accepted so that
families could swim together as well as paddle. The bathing-
machines gave way to tents or to fixed beach huts above the high-
tide mark. If a family could not afford to hire a beach hut they
could undress on the beach behind a canvas wind-break or a
towel. The perambulating beach entertainers moved into the new
winter-gardens or theatres. The hawkers of food and drink
moved into arcades or shops on the promenade. There were still
a few ice-cream sellers, peanut vendors and candy-floss and hot-
dog stands on the beach, although by the 1930s many of these
had changed over to pedal tricycles with deep boxes for their
wares, rather than the shoulder-slung boxes or baskets of their
predecessors, and did not go on to the beach itself.

Life at the seaside has been recorded almost from its beginning, firstly in the prints and engravings of the late eighteenth
century, then in the fashion prints of the nineteenth century. The
Victorian seaside was caricatured by the cartoonists, notably by
John Leech, who was a contributor to *Punch,* and painted by
artists, among them William Frith RA, William Dyce RA,
Augustus Egg and Philip Wilson Steer.

From the beginnings of photography the seaside was used as a
subject, first for its scenic beauty, with no people in sight, then,
by 1860, with small figures, often deliberately posed. Studio
photographers flourished in the seaside towns and many
holidaymakers took home a carte-de-visite as a souvenir, while
from the 1880s itinerant photographers would take portraits on
the beach, developing them on the spot.

The invention of the roll film by George Eastman in 1888
enabled middle-class families to take their own holiday photographs. The first roll-film cameras had to be returned to the
manufacturers, Kodak, for developing and printing; the owners
received the camera back with a new film in it ready to expose,

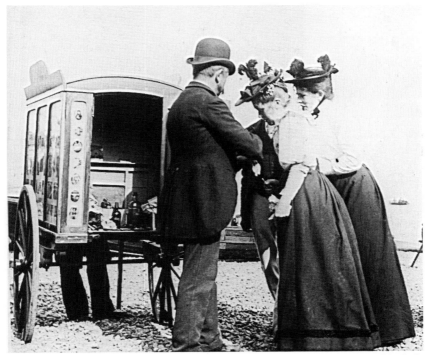

8. *Mr Berrecloth, the tintype photographer at Hastings in 1895, with his portable dark-room on a hand-cart. He wears respectable lower middle-class clothes. His clients, who may well be day trippers, wear dark skirts, white blouses and decorated hats.*

and the prints from their exposed film. These cameras had one hundred exposures on each roll of film. They were expensive but with their advent photography became available to many people who were not interested in its mechanics but only in the pictures it produced. Even royalty could now record the lives of their own families and Princess Alexandra, later Queen Alexandra, was an accomplished photographer.

Daylight loading roll film was available by the late 1890s and photography gradually became cheaper and easier until by the 1930s the Box Brownie camera had made snapshot photography available to all. This book sets out to show the changing fashions of life at the seaside as recorded by the camera (with a little help from the artists).

9. *A holiday couple at Cliftonville, Kent, in 1922. The young man is wearing plus-fours with a matching jacket and waistcoat. The young woman wears a darker-coloured suit. The weather, although sunny, appears to be none too warm, for she is wearing a long cardigan under her jacket as well as a fashionable fox fur round her shoulders. She holds a box camera and smiles at the friend who is taking her photograph (probably with a similar camera), and who is completely unaware that her shadow, falling on the people she is photographing, reveals that she is wearing a hat like that of the girl in the picture.*

2. Holidaymakers' clothes up to 1860

Bathing-costumes

The first enthusiasts for sea-bathing, as prescribed by doctors of the seventeenth and eighteenth centuries, were probably naked, although no surviving early print shows figures on a beach in sufficient detail to determine their sex or what they wore. Written descriptions of eighteenth-century Scarborough tell us that the men, jumping from boats a little way out to sea, wore no clothes, while the women, at the edge of the waves, wore long flannel shifts with long sleeves. Children did not bathe. These descriptions would probably have applied equally to all other early seaside watering places.

As most bathing was done in the early morning, winter or summer, a waiting-room was usually provided where coffee could be purchased and newspapers read while waiting one's turn for the bathing-machine. Nobody lingered on the beach itself, before or after bathing, until well into the nineteenth century. In many towns men and women met in the beach waiting-room and took their turn in the bathing-machine, regardless of sex. Bathing itself was not a pleasure; usually it was no more than a quick but complete immersion, with women attendants who made sure that the bather went completely under the water.

By Regency times, 1811-20, bathing had begun to be a pleasure in the summer. Even earlier, about 1802, young Elizabeth Ham recorded in her diary that she enjoyed her bathing and that her bathing-dress was made of green baize.

As bathing became more of a pleasure, women's bathing-dresses gradually became shorter, in some cases losing their sleeves too, until by the 1840s they were aptly described as sacks turned upside-down with holes for the head and arms to go through. Some women even managed to swim quite well in these garments. Under these sacks they were naked, and as most of them merely sat at the edge of the water and let the waves roll over them or bobbed about in the sea by the steps of the bathing-machines there were many articles published in the newspapers about the indecency of bathing-dresses which the action of the water could carry up to the wearer's armpits 'so she might as well be without a dress at all!'

Beach and promenade clothes

Out of the water the clothes worn on the beach in the early nineteenth century reflected the current fashion, for the seaside

A MERMAID.

10 (left). *A fashion print from La Belle Assemblée for 1st August 1814. The garment is described as a 'Circassian ladies' corset and seaside bathing-dress, invented and to be had exclusively from Mrs Bell, no. 20, Charlotte Street, Bedford Square, London'. This garment may be the kind that Elizabeth Ham wore, although we may wonder if anyone actually went into the sea in this outfit, or if they took off the top layer and wore only the under part into the water.*

11 (right). *There are no photographs of bathing-dresses in the 1850s. This drawing by John Leech shows the 'bottomless sack' type of bathing-dress worn by the majority of women who ventured into the water. It also depicts the folding canopy over the seaward door of the bathing-machine, a canopy that had much in common with the crinolines the bathers wore when not in the water. Note the neat cap worn by the bather and the length of the dress as hinted at in the figure about to come down the steps.*

town was a place in which to be seen as much as to see. Sea-air, not the sun, was what was considered beneficial. Sunburn was to be avoided at all costs. From the 1840s onward London shopkeepers were advertising clothes and accessories for the seaside. Veils to be worn when promenading were offered by Dison's the lace merchant, while other London shops were selling 'seaside paletots' (coats) and 'Scarborough suits', both expressly designed for wear at the seaside. The women's fashion magazines ran regular articles in June, July and August on clothes for the seaside.

Today we think of the beach as a place where one wears less clothing than usual but in the 1840s the beach was enlivened by

colourful clothes of all kinds; a young woman sitting or walking
on the beach would wear far more clothes than she would wear to
a dance in the evening. For men it was an opportunity to wear
various forms of 'fancy dress'; these could range from a checked
'lounging' jacket and a matelot hat up to a 'Turkish' style costume of full trousers strapped in at the ankles and a turban-
shaped hat. None of these clothes would have been considered
respectable in either town or countryside, but beside the sea they
were taken as a matter of course.

One other consideration was applied to fashionable seaside
costume in the first half of the nineteenth century: it was considered ephemeral and was therefore made of cheaper fabrics
and materials than everyday or formal clothes; the clothes advertised for the seaside were commended for their inexpensiveness
as well as for their stylishness and suitability for holiday wear.
Most of these early seaside fashions lasted only a season and
were then discarded, not because they were unfashionable but
because sun, sea-air and salt in bad weather ruined cheap
clothes. How much so is revealed in the diary for 1837 of William
Taylor, a footman, visiting Brighton with the family for whom he
worked; he recorded that, after watching rough seas on a stormy
day in August, 'My hat is as white as though I had rolled it in the
salt tub'.

12. *In 1875 Captain Matthew Webb became the first
man to swim the English Channel from England to
France. It took him 21 hours 45 minutes, and a
drawing of him, made at the time, showed him wearing
a garment that could have been made out of a
Victorian man's singlet with short sleeves. It resembled
the costume of a French acrobat, Jules Leotard, and
such a one-piece close-fitting garment was adopted by
serious Victorian male swimmers as their 'regulation'
costume. This example, from an old swimming in-
struction book first published in Victorian times,
differs from that worn by Captain Webb only in-
asmuch as the Captain's costume had short sleeves.*

13. *A carte-de-visite published by John C. Twyman and Son in 1863. They had studios in Margate and Ramsgate and this picture shows the beach below the pier in one of these resorts. The holidaymakers on the beach sit on plain wooden upright chairs — the deck-chair is not yet in use on beaches — and no one is wearing a bathing-dress. Bathing is strictly regulated and confined to bathing-machines on special parts of the beach. The women wear spreading crinoline-supported skirts, long-sleeved jackets and small hats if they are young, bonnets if they are older. Several women carry large umbrellas, here used to keep off the sun. There are more women than men sitting on the beach, but more men than women on the pier. The blurred patches represent people who have moved about during the exposure. The man on the promenade (bottom left), looking down on the beach, is wearing an early straw hat.*

3. Holidaymakers' clothes 1860-80

Beach and bathing costumes: men

Most seaside resorts allocated different parts of the beach for male and female bathing, and by 1850 not only were the sexes segregated by areas but also by times, men being permitted to bathe only in the early hours of the morning and in the evenings, to avoid public indecency. The moralists had protested against the practice of nude male swimming from the early years of the century; their athletic protagonists had equally vigorously defended it as being healthy, and the arguments were to continue until the 1870s.

Bathing-costumes for men had existed since the 1830s, originating in France, where mixed bathing had been normal since the late eighteenth century. These early costumes were simply very short-legged drawers, called *caleçons,* held up by a string at the waist. They appeared in England in the 1840s and were available to male bathers who hired bathing-machines. They hired a machine, the use of a towel and drawers. Many Englishmen hated them, considering them effeminate or, worse still, dangerous. They could fall off as a bather came out of the sea and trip him up on the stones of the beach. These drawers were very conspicuous, for they were striped in broad bands, red and white being the most common colours. Perhaps this was the real reason most Englishmen disliked them. But the practice of wearing such swimming drawers gradually took hold. The men's beaches in the 1860s would have revealed half the men (probably the older ones) naked while the other half wore drawers.

In the late 1850s swimming began to be taken seriously, both as an exercise and as a possible means of saving life. Swimming clubs for young men were formed. One of the earliest was in Brighton in 1858, with an entrance fee of one shilling and a subscription of twopence a week. Soon swimming became a sport and the Brighton Swimming Club held its first races in 1861. All competitors were warned that they would not be allowed to compete unless they wore swimming drawers.

Because drawers held up by a cord could fall down, a one-piece costume for men was being made and sold by the 1870s. This, too, may have originated in France, for it resembled the French fisherman's short-sleeved, horizontally striped jersey with the bottom cut into short legs. Certainly it was worn in France, for it appears in French cartoons showing mixed bathing. In these 1870 cartoons the men all wear striped bathing-costumes

14. *A sketch made by John Leech at Scarborough in about 1865, showing the informal clothes of the holidaymakers and the more formal dress of the groom (who may also be the family coachman) leading the pony ridden by a teenage girl.*

and the women plain dark-coloured garments. By 1870 English proprietors of bathing-machines also hired out one-piece bathing-costumes for men.

When not swimming, people on the beach or promenading in the town wore their best and most fashionable clothes. They were on holiday and did not want to wear anything resembling their working dress. The day trippers would put on their newest clothes to make the most of their brief holiday. Away from their normal work, the labourers and artisans tried to look like clerks or shop assistants. The young clerks and shop assistants tried to look like students, actors or military officers on leave. It was a great game, to lay claim to a status higher or other than their own. Clothes for holiday wear were no longer advertised for their cheapness but for their suitability for a holiday, and this required them to make a good, as well as a fashionable, impression.

If a man was so well off that he did not need to make an impression on others or pretend to a higher status, he wore comfortable informal wear. In the 1860s this consisted of the lounge-suit: trousers, waistcoat and a hip-length jacket made in the same fabric. It was originally what its name implies, casual wear, for those whose normal clothes were formal dress. In 1864, for young men who wanted a different kind of wear at the seaside,

15. *Adults riding donkeys beside the sea. The man wears a tweed lounge-suit and a hard hat; the fashionable young lady with shoulder epaulettes and a pert little hat is riding side-saddle on her donkey with her crinoline cage bunched at each side.*

Minister's *Gazette of Fashion* recommended 'a short jacket and moderately full knickerbockers'. This was to become the uniform of the cyclist in the next decade but was popular as a walking costume as well as a seaside one in the 1860s.

By the 1870s most men at the seaside would have worn three-piece lounge-suits. With these suits they would have worn a shirt, with a collar and tie, and a hat of one kind or another. Sunbathing was not considered at all, and fashionable and middle-class men preferred not to become tanned by the sun. Only those who worked out of doors would be sun-tanned, and even these men uncovered as little of their skins to the sun as possible.

The 'fancy dress' of the first half of the nineteenth century had disappeared by the 1870s. However, there were some new ideas that were first introduced at the seaside, and one of the most popular and long-lasting of these more practical fashions is the canvas shoe with rubber sole. Originally known as 'sand shoes', they were invented in 1868 and rapidly became popular for wear on the beach by men, women and children. In 1876 they were nicknamed 'plimsolls'; for in that year the manufacturers decided to strengthen them by putting a line of rubber up over the canvas of the shoe. This line was likened to that marked on the hulls of ships to indicate their loading level under the Merchant Shipping Act of 1876, adopted through the campaigning of Samuel Plim-

16. *A detail from an early outdoor carte-de-visite, probably sold as a souvenir, of Anstey's Cove, near Torquay. The two figures standing on the beach are fully clothed in walking dress, the man in long coat, trousers and a small hat, the woman in a skirt hitched up over a spreading crinoline. Her jacket is long and loose and her hat has a pork-pie shape. Also in the picture is another woman, sitting with her back to a rock, looking at the other two. She is wearing a shawl over her shoulders and a straw hat with long dark ribbons hanging down the back.*

soll. 'Plimsolls', as a name for this type of shoe, has passed into the English language and the same style of shoe can still be bought today. During the nineteenth century they were probably the only casual style of outdoor shoe available.

Beach and bathing-costumes: women and children

The 1850s and early 1860s were a period of emancipation for women, not least through the invention of the cage crinoline. Although men did not like it and the cartoonists caricatured it unmercifully, the majority of women wore it happily. It had several advantages. Firstly, the wide-spread skirt made every waist look smaller, so doing away with the necessity for very tight lacing; secondly, it superseded the layers of petticoats, up to nine or more, which had been needed to hold out the full skirts of the 1830s and early 1840s. Freed from the weight of these petticoats, wearing hoops which did not constrict the legs and corsets which did not have to be pulled in so tightly, the younger women became much more active. 'Fast young ladies' was the description applied to the 'sporting' girls of the mid nineteenth century who, wearing crinolines, played croquet, rode donkeys at the seaside, set off for long walks and even climbed mountains, generally showing an independence that scandalised their parents.

Walking dresses or sports clothes of this period had either

THE FASHIONS
Expressly designed & prepared
for the
Englishwoman's Domestic Magazine.

17 (left). *A young woman in a carte-de-visite of 1862, taken by J. C. Paterson of Alnwick in Northumberland. Although this is not a seaside photograph it shows very clearly the clothes that would have been worn at the time for walking, either on the moors or on the beach. It also shows the way the skirt hitched up to reveal the shorter crinoline petticoat.*

18 (right). *A fashion print of September 1864 showing the fashions recommended for the seaside in that year. The skirt would drag on the ground when not hitched up. Striped fabrics, whether used for the whole dress, for a petticoat or just as a trimming, have always been popular for holiday wear.*

skirts short enough to show the ankles or were made to be hitched up over a coloured (often scarlet) petticoat. This hitching up was achieved by concealed cords which could be pulled up to gather up the lower part of the skirt, thus giving freedom to the feet. A music-hall song of 1860 describes this fashion and its wearers:

> 'Skirts hitched up on spreading frame
> Petticoats as bright as flame
> Dandy high-heeled boots proclaim
> The Fast Young Ladies.'

Sometimes the revealed petticoats were striped red and white or blue and white; sometimes they were made of white *broderie anglaise*. The fashion writers advised on suitable fabrics for seaside clothes. Strong washable cottons, serge and even tweed were advocated; silk and soft woollens were not considered appropriate. White piqué, trimmed with black or coloured braids, was a popular choice for seaside promenade dresses, so was muslin, which could have a printed pattern on it or be woven with a satin stripe or check. As the seaside was usually more windy than elsewhere, jackets of various lengths from waist to knee were worn over the dresses, rather than the shawls of the previous decade.

In the 1850s bonnets had been women's normal headwear, but from 1860 onward younger women began to wear wide-brimmed straw hats, particularly in the countryside or at the seaside. These could be tied on with long scarves if necessary. For highly fashionable wear small 'pill-box' or pork-pie hats gradually became popular.

In 1852 Mrs Amelia Bloomer, an American, had invented a new style of dress for domestic wear, an outfit based on that worn by patients in a Swiss sanatorium. This consisted of long full trousers gathered in at the ankles, a knee-length skirt, a blouse and a jacket. In the Swiss hospitals it was worn by the patients without corsets under it, thus giving their lungs the best opportunity to recover from the ravages of tuberculosis or over-tight lacing. Amelia Bloomer also campaigned for the abandonment of tight lacing. For all her travels and lectures advocating her new-style clothes they never became an everyday fashion, although some women did wear them, both in the United States and Britain. By the mid 1860s even Mrs Bloomer had gone back to wearing a conventional crinoline-skirted dress.

Her design had been adopted enthusiastically by the French, however, as a bathing-costume. Their version was slightly simpler than the day wear designed by Amelia Bloomer, for the French bathing-dress consisted of ankle-length trousers gathered at the ankles, topped by a knee-length or thigh-length jacket. There were no underclothes and the jacket or tunic was usually short-sleeved. The whole outfit was much more respectable than the knee-length sacks which had preceded it, and, judging by the fashion-plates of the day, some of these bathing-dresses were very pretty indeed, for they were made of a dark-coloured fabric, which could be flannel or serge, trimmed with braid and embroidery. Blue or red were very popular colours. Lace-up slippers could be worn with a bathing-dress if the beach were stony.

By the early 1860s the bloomer suit had become the standard women's bathing-costume on all the beaches of France and the British Isles. In this outfit it was possible, at last, for women to learn to swim properly. Swimming instructors were employed by the owners of the bathing-machines and lessons could be arranged; most of these instructors were men. The women 'dippers' who had reigned on the beaches since the end of the eighteenth century, insisting that bathers put their heads under the water, became little more than bathing-hut attendants.

By the 1860s people had begun to use the beach for recreation as well as for actual bathing. As a result of this families went together to the beach and children began to play on it. The people of the early nineteenth century had considered riding one of the attractions of the seaside, but this had been horse-riding, usually on the downs behind the early seaside towns. In the 1850s donkeys and donkey-riding had been introduced to English beaches and by the 1860s were an established part of the seaside. At first adults had ridden donkeys, and the cartoonists had included the donkey ride in their list of unsuitable activities for young women in crinolines. However, donkey-riding soon became almost a monopoly of children, who have been pictured by cartoonists riding donkeys on beaches in their everyday clothes. The little girls wore short knee-length crinoline dresses, short jackets and brimmed hats; the little boys wore knee-length knickerbocker suits decorated with braid. In these clothes they also ran races on the beaches and dug with toy wooden spades using buckets to mould castles out of the sand.

In the late 1850s Queen Victoria dressed her young sons in summer in a version of the matelot sailor's dress, but with short trousers. This dress included the wide collar worn by sailors and the necktie that passed under it to tie in front. Whatever the royal children wore rapidly became fashionable and the 'sailor suits' were soon fashionable summer wear for small boys of all social classes. By the late 1860s sailor suits were boys' standard summer wear and were to remain popular seaside wear for boys — and as time went on for girls, too, although with skirts rather than trousers — until well into the twentieth century.

Young children were taken bathing by their mothers and older sisters rather than by their fathers, and therefore small boys would have worn bathing drawers. These small boys of the late 1850s were the young men of the 1860s and 1870s who wore first bathing drawers and then one-piece costumes, while their fathers and grandfathers were still bathing naked. Little girls wore bathing-costumes like their mothers, but their trousers were wide and knee-length under their tunics. As these little girls began to grow up in the 1870s they went on wearing straight knee-length

19 (left). *A small boy dressed ready for the beach in the late 1860s. He wears a tweed suit of knickerbockers and collarless jacket, both lavishly embroidered with a couched-down braiding. The sleeves of his jacket have buttons on them. His shirt has a turn-down collar and a neat tie, crossed in front and fastened with a pin or stud. He is probably about four or five years old and wears mid-calf-length socks and buttoned boots. His hat is a plain round straw hat.*

20 (right). *A dark sailor suit of the 1870s over a white back-fastening blouse with a dark (probably blue) edging instead of a collar. The boy's lanyard is threaded through a loop on the front of his jacket and fastens to his middle button. He wears a plain round straw hat with a dangling ribbon, but over his dark socks he wears ankle-strap shoes. Although he carries a bucket and spade ready for the beach he also wears a large flower with leaves set round it pinned to his chest. Perhaps the photograph was to be a special present for a grandparent. Perhaps this was his first sailor suit after wearing the dresses of babyhood. Certainly this style of shoe denoted a very young child.*

trousers to their bathing-costumes rather than the ankle-length gathered 'bloomers' worn by their mothers. By the end of the 1870s only older women wore gathered long trousers as part of their bathing-dress.

The trimmings on girls' bathing-dresses matched those of their mothers. Light grey serge trimmed with red worsted braid, or brown holland (a coarse linen fabric) trimmed with white braid, or even mid-blue flannel trimmed with red, white and blue ribbons was considered suitable for girls' bathing-costumes. Practically any dark colour could be used for bathing clothes, but white and pale pink were considered unsuitable as they became transparent when wet. Most bathing-dresses were advertised as 'not showing the figure when wet'.

The cut of the neckline and the decoration of the upper part of the bathing-costume followed daytime fashionable wear for both women and girls. Epaulettes on the shoulder seams were fashionable in day dresses and so were also fashionable on bathing-dresses in the 1860s. Both day and bathing-dresses of this period had plain round necks. Contrasting yokes, or trimmings suggesting a yoke, were popular in the 1870s both on day and bathing-dresses. Sailor collars were also popular on bathing-dresses from 1870.

The fashion writers of the 1870s became quite lyrical over bathing-costumes. In 1870 they recommended 'drawers fastened below the knee with scarlet ribbon'. These were to be worn under a basque jacket with short puffed sleeves. In 1874 the reommendation was for 'drawers topped by a tunic with a waist-belt and deep sailor collar'; by 1877 deep pink and blue flannel were the fashionable colours and fabric, but cotton bunting was also recommended as being durable. In 1878 the recommendation was for a costume 'in the form of combinations with a short, separate overskirt'.

Bathing shoes for the 1860s and 1870s were like flat ballet shoes tied on with ribbons wound round the ankles.

For the rest of the holiday at the seaside both women and children wore fashionable outdoor day dress. A seaside holiday involved sightseeing and being seen; therefore, clothes were always governed by convention, even in the most 'informal' situations. High necks, stiff corsets and even dragging trains are seen on the fashion-plates suggesting suitable seaside wear. By 1870 the crinoline disappeared in favour of the bustle and train, a fashion in which it was difficult to look 'sporting' or casual. It was possible, however, if the popular 'double skirt' style of dress was

21. Bathing-dresses of 1871 showing a mother in a bloomer-type bathing-dress with trousers gathered at the ankles, and her daughters in wide-legged short trousers under thigh-length overdresses. Decorative braid trimming, as on the adult's bathing-dress, was also fashionable on day dresses of the time.

worn, for a walking dress could still be fashionable without a train if it had a neat overskirt, draped at the back. This style owed much to the clothes worn by the Newhaven fishwives, a striped underskirt and dark overskirt. A 'fishwife' style outfit was the heart's desire of many small girls. They wore it with short skirts but their older sisters wore long skirts with draped apron-like overskirts. In these clothes the older girls often wore their hair long and loose as a sign of informality. All formal occasions demanded that grown women's hair was firmly 'put up' in whatever style of chignon or braiding was fashionable at the time. Both 'fishwife' dresses and sailor suits with knee-length skirts were worn on beaches by young teenagers and small girls in the 1870s. Norfolk jackets for women, made in the same style as a man's Norfolk coat jacket, appeared in 1877 and these were worn with long pleated skirts by older teenagers and young women. They were particularly useful for cold days. The sun does not always shine at the seaside.

4. Holidaymakers' clothes 1880-1900

By the 1880s the moralists and the fashion-conscious had won the argument about nude bathing. It was no longer permitted. By-laws were drafted, printed and displayed on beaches all round Britain, declaring that all persons, male and female, should wear bathing-costumes that covered them from neck to knee and that these costumes should be made of material that prevented 'indecent exposure of the figure when wet'. Bathing was still a segregated pastime, no male 'over the age of eight years' being permitted to bathe with the women and girls or even to approach within a specified number of yards of a bathing-machine used by women. Conversely, the women were not allowed near machines used by men. Bathing-machines were strictly controlled and bathing without using a machine in which to change was either forbidden or allowed only at specified times and in specified places.

Families walked, played and sat on the beach in the last two decades of the nineteenth century, but they did not normally do so in their bathing-costumes, which were kept strictly for bathing.

Bathing-costumes: men

Men's bathing-costumes were similar to those worn in the 1870s. They were usually one-piece costumes with knee-length legs and short sleeves. The neck was wide enough for the whole costume to be put on by being drawn upward over the body. A high-necked costume could be buttoned down the chest. These costumes were usually made of a knitted, rather thin, cotton fabric often striped red and white, although plain dark blue, black or maroon costumes were available and were worn by serious swimmers. As in the 1870s many proprietors of bathing-machines hired out swimming costumes to men.

In the 1890s some variations on the one-piece costume appeared. Although still made in one piece, the lower half could be plain and the top striped. It was also possible for men to obtain and wear two-piece costumes: drawers to cover the lower part of the body and a jersey to cover the chest. While most of these would have been made of a knitted fabric, a few 1890s pictures show men in two-piece costumes that, from their cut and hang, appear to be made of a woven fabric — serge or flannel — similar to that used for women's bathing-costumes. Conversely some of the candid camera photographs taken by the photographer Paul Martin on the island of Jersey in 1893 show older

22. A man in a two-piece bathing-costume cut in a similar style to those worn by the girls, but with a jersey-style top probably buttoning at the neck rather than all the way down as a jacket. The boy in the picture is wearing a knee-length one-piece bathing costume. This is one of a set of stereoscope pictures depicting people at the seaside in the 1890s.

men in the water, or about to dive in, wearing the very briefest of stockinette bathing drawers. It would appear that the choice of men's costumes was quite wide and that some resorts were stricter in enforcing the bylaws than others; since no one sat about the beach in their bathing-costumes, there are comparatively few photographs taken in England showing men, or women for that matter, in bathing-costumes out of the water before the turn of the century. Cartoons, however, were plentiful, and show that boys often wore knee-length bathing drawers rather than full costumes.

Bathing-costumes: women and children

The new-style bathing-costume in the form of a one-piece garment with knee-length legs and elbow-length sleeves introduced in the late 1870s was, without its detachable overskirt, almost identical to that worn by men. It was made at first of a woven rather than a knitted fabric. But the fashion ideal in 1880 was for an extremely slim outline, with the bodice of dresses cut to resemble the corset worn beneath them. The bodices of evening-dresses almost looked as if the woman was wearing only a corset and petticoat. It is not perhaps surprising that in 1880 some women wore a bathing-costume that resembled a pair of colour-ed knee-length combinations with a matching corset over the top, the 'skirt' being reduced to no more than a waist frill or a sash fastened only on one hip. Others wore a combination suit with an overskirt and as wide a corselet belt as possible, thus achieving almost the appearance of a corset. These corseted costumes were known as 'bathing stays' and were fashionable for perhaps only two or three years. But the one-piece costume with an overskirt went on into the 1890s alongside the older two-piece costume of drawers and jacket which continued to be worn by those who found it more comfortable. In 1880 this was often made of dark grey serge, trimmed with white braid and worn with a red woollen sash and a straw hat. These straw hats were also a new fashion in 1880 and were usually shallow-crowned and wide-brimmed, held on by a wide ribbon passing over the crown and tying behind the head at the nape of the neck under a bun of hair. This tipped the hat forward over the eyes, thus shading the face from any possible sunburn. Straw-soled shoes with linen uppers, looking like short boots with cut-away scalloped fronts, laced or

23. *A fashion-plate of the 1880s showing the type of bathing-dress that was current for women and girls. All these designs are of drawers and a long tunic. Note the hats; even the child wears a hat tipped forward over her face. One of the women has a large white towelling wrap over her bathing-dress.*

24 and 25. *Two stereoscope pictures of about 1899, part of a series depicting people at the seaside. In the left-hand picture, the three girls are wearing bathing-dresses that consist of knee-length drawers and jackets trimmed with white braid. One girl's drawers are gathered into a band at the knee; the others are loose and edged with braid. In the right-hand picture, the girl about to dive into the water, following a companion, wears a separate, almost knee-length skirt over a one-piece combination costume. She wears black stockings and shoes with her bathing-dress.*

buttoned at wide intervals, were another innovation of 1880 and were worn in the water to protect the feet. Most bathers, however, still wore plain slippers, like ballet shoes, held on by lacing around the ankles.

The *Girls' Own Paper*, a magazine for young women, regularly published articles on dress and fashion. The issue of 27th September 1884 included several paragraphs on the subject of clothes for the seaside, including bathing-dresses. Of these, the writer (anonymous but described as 'A Lady Dressmaker') states that there are only two shapes, 'the combination trousers and corsage worn with a belt and short tunic' and 'the trousers, made separately, and the upper part in blouse shape with a band'. At this time a 'tunic' meant a short overskirt, and a 'blouse' meant a garment falling to the thigh. A 'band' was a belt. The writer goes on to say: 'Blue and red cottons or thick cretonnes are new materials, the latter being trimmed, as well as the former, with coarse lace. Then some young ladies who are good swimmers have adopted the striped woollen jersey of the fisherman and wear it with full knickerbockers of blue serge.'

Swimming clubs for girls started in the late 1880s, competitive swimming soon becoming one of their activities.

Blue serge seems to have been the most popular material for seaside bathing-dresses, flannel being condemned as it soaked up the water, adding weight to the costume. As in the 1860s and 1870s bathing-dresses were trimmed with white braid and could have a white sailor collar with a 'modesty' piece covering the upper chest. An alternative to the white braid was red; turkey-red twilled cloth was used for sashes and belts. All bathing-dresses had high necks at the beginning of the 1880s but these became lower while the sleeves slowly became shorter until by 1890 they were practically sleeveless. From 1893, however, sleeves of dresses and coats began to get larger. In 1894 they were at their largest and leg-of-mutton shaped. In 1895 this changed to a sleeve that was tight on the forearm but formed a very large puffed sleeve on the upper arm. In the second half of the 1890s bathing-dresses had low square necks but very large puffed sleeves covering the upper arm.

The straw hats of the 1870s and 1880s gave way to mob-caps or turbans worn in the water. As girls began to swim seriously these caps and turbans were designed to help keep the hair dry rather than shade the face. *The Housewife* of 1894 carried an article which read: 'For those who indulge in bathing and swimming some manufacturers have invented a charming bathing cap. It is called "The Normandy" and is intended to be worn by girls on the sands and as a speciality or distinguishing badge for club swimmers and those who compete in swimming contests. It is pretty and quaint and is made in satin in all the art shades. The front forms a box-pleated frill, eminently becoming to the face of the wearer. The outline both of pleats and curtain, is bound with brocaded ribbon of contrasting tints to the main portion of the cap. Strings of brocade tie the cap into position under the chin. These caps are also made in satin with india-rubber linings, also in delightful patterns of sateen, with trimmings and bows of fancy or self-coloured ribbon. The different colours are intended as badges for swimming clubs and competitions.' The same article also recommended 'a round bathing cap, without strings, made in pink, yellow or white jaconet, in check twill, turkey-red twill, fancy sateen, ordinary check, silk in various tints and some few other fabrics'. Jaconet was a thin cotton fabric with a waterproof backing. The sketch which accompanied this description showed a cap similar to a mob-cap, but without its frill. The 'Normandy' cap was a mob-cap with a pleated frill.

26. *A 'pin-up' picture of the mid 1890s showing bathing beauties in elaborate bathing-dresses, knee-length drawers and stockings, posing on the steps of a bathing-machine. The bodices and sleeves of these costumes follow the fashionable lines of day dresses of the time, even to the high collars and shaped belts. It is doubtful if anyone attempted serious swimming in a bathing-dress like this. Most real bathing-dresses would have been far simpler versions of this kind of style. While a real bathing-dress would have had a modesty vest filling in the plunging neckline, few women would have worn a high-necked long-sleeved undergarment beneath it as depicted here. These bathers are definitely overdressed, even by the standards of their own time.*

The English fashion drawings and cartoons of the early 1890s show girls and women bare-legged from the knee down and bare-footed, but in the United States long black stockings and slip-on shoes were worn on the beach and in the water. The United States, like France, allowed mixed bathing, and an American woman, writing in an English magazine in 1893, commented on her surprise to see bare legs and feet at the English seaside. She suggested that Englishwomen, too, should wear long black stockings. 'You have no idea how decent they make the whole proceeding.' By 1900 many Englishwomen took to wearing long black stockings with their bathing-dresses.

Beachwear and promenade costume: men

During the 1880s a new style of jacket became popular as sports and seaside wear for men. This was the blazer, a double-breasted box-shaped jacket made of striped flannel. At first it was laughed at and caricatured in the music halls as the extreme of informality, for it resembled a pyjama jacket. But it was comfortable and practical; once adopted, the blazer became the conventional jacket to denote an informal summer occasion. It was worn at cricket matches by players and spectators, at tennis matches, on the river, in boats and at the seaside. A blazer could be striped in any number or combination of colours including black and white. It could be as vivid, as loud and vulgar or as discreetly coloured in dark tones as the wearer chose. By the 1890s blazers were almost a uniform at the seaside.

The wearer of a blazer could dispense with a waistcoat; for the first time in the nineteenth century it became permissible for men to appear without one. For sporting activities many older men replaced waistcoats with wide cummerbunds, worn over the shirt and braces, under the blazer, but young men and boys wore no braces, holding up their trousers with a wide canvas belt, often fastened with a buckle that resembled an S laid on its side. This S buckle continued into the twentieth century as part of the schoolboy's belt. The belts were often striped in two colours, the stripes running horizontally round the wearer's waist. Short neckties became associated with sport and were therefore also worn at the seaside. Although a blazer and belt denoted informality, no man would appear without a collar and tie, even on the beach, much less on the promenade or pier, and neither would they appear without a hat.

The hat that dominated the 1890s was the straw boater. It had started in the 1870s as sportswear (usually for boating, hence the

27. *A teenage boy photographed while on holiday at Margate in the 1890s. He wears a blazer, a boater, a short tie and a belt with a snake buckle. These were the sports and holiday clothes of the fashionable young man.*

nickname 'boater') but by the late 1870s and 1880s it had become the normal hat for summer wear. The straw hat had become even more of a uniform than the middle classes' blazer, for it could be worn with a lounge-suit or artisan's working clothes even in the town in summer. These straw hats were flat-topped with brims between 2 and 3 inches (50-75 mm) wide. The sides of the hat were circled by a ribbon which could be plain or striped. The straw hat transcended class and sex, for young women and girls wore it as well, in all circumstances except the most formal. However, popular though the straw boater was, many photographs of the 1890s show older men at the seaside wearing bowler hats, while other men and boys favoured flat caps.

28. *Fishing from the beach somewhere on the south coast in 1899. The man holding the rod wears a white shirt and trousers with a black bow tie and a cummerbund. He also wears a plain dark blazer and a straw boater. A cummerbund was an acceptable alternative to a waistcoat when engaged in outdoor leisure activity and was therefore appropriate beach wear for this middle-aged man. His two companions wear medium-brimmed hats decorated with ribbons and having small spotted veils hanging from the brims. Veils and gloves were often worn by women sitting on a beach for the same reason that parasols or umbrellas were carried — to keep the sun from their skin. Both these women wear blouses with leg-of-mutton sleeves, which were first fashionable five years before this photograph was taken.*

Beach and promenade wear: women

The highlight of the seaside holiday for many women was not the dip in the sea but the daily promenade on the road along the top of the beach or on the pier. One had to pay to go on to the pier and, at least until the 1920s, it was considered a place for formality in dress. Here, in the 1880s, women could show off their new holiday dresses, all of which had bustles, while many had trains as well, dragging over the boards of the pier deck. Blue and white were fashionable colours for seaside dresses, but a writer in the *Girls' Own Paper* for September 1884 also recommended black lace over grey silk. Dresses without trains had either accordion-pleated skirts or fairly narrow skirts with rows of tucks round the bottom; most dresses had draped overskirts. However, a new style of clothes for women was developing during the 1880s; this was the tailored suit, consisting of a plain skirt and hip-length jacket, worn over a blouse. By the 1890s the bustle had disappeared, leaving women in plain skirts emphasised only by narrow waists achieved by corseting. Since fashion seems to abhor the normal, sleeves, especially the upper sleeve, became bigger and bigger in the mid 1890s. This fashion for large sleeves influenced not only day dresses, tailored suits and evening-dresses, but, as has already been noted, bathing-dresses as well.

All through the Victorian period daytime necklines were always high to the throat. Even seaside dresses and blouses did

29 (left). *A fashion-plate for seaside dresses for 1881 features narrow skirts trimmed with layers of frills, lace, gauging and ribbons. The tight-fitting cuirass bodices emphasise the waist while the skirts are looped up and held back with many swathes of different fabrics. The fashionable hair style has a short curly fringe. The child's dress has a very long bodice and a very short skirt.*

30 (right). *The reality of seaside fashions in the 1880s at Southsea, Portsmouth, where two young women pose in the studio of W. J. Robinson; a mast and rigging give a nautical setting. Their dresses are fashionable for the mid 1880s and their skirts give them much more room in which to move than those in the fashion-plate. These girls both wear pleated underskirts with overskirts drawn up at the back on a bustle foundation. The girl on the left has a striped belt, cuffs and collar to her dark dress, while the girl on the right has a striped underskirt and bodice with the same striped fabric used for the cuffs of her jacket. Both have fashionable curly fringes. Both these dresses, with their 'short' (three-quarter-length) sleeves, could have been worn on the beach. Pleated skirts did not have trains to drag on the ground.*

31. *A fashion-plate showing clothes for children in 1880. The girls' dresses have long bodices and very short skirts. Tight ankle boots are also worn by the little girls in the drawing. The girls, like the adults, have fashionable curly fringes with longer back hair; girls' hair was left loose or tied back with a ribbon while adults' hair was put in a chignon. Both the older girls wear hats trimmed with ribbon. One of the boys in the picture wears a sailor suit and a straw hat; the other boy (bottom right, sailing a boat in a pool) wears a knickerbocker suit with a long belted tunic instead of a jacket.*

not relax this rule. On a fine warm day in the 1890s a woman could take off her jacket and promenade in her skirt and blouse; in this she had an advantage over the men, for men could not and did not promenade in their shirt sleeves, although a few, probably only the working class, took their jackets off on the beach and sat down in their shirts, waistcoats and hats. As in earlier days, nobody courted a suntan: the women always wore hats out of doors even on the beach and they quite often carried parasols as well to shield their faces from the sun.

Beach and promenade wear: children

On the beach children wore their ordinary clothes and always something covering their head. However, children's clothes became increasingly practical during the 1880s. Girls as well as boys wore sailor suits, the girls with short skirts, the boys with short or long trousers according to their age. In addition both sexes discovered the comfort and ease of the fisherman's jersey and the knitted 'brewer's cap' worn with skirt or trousers. Compared to the layers of clothing worn by little girls in the 1860s and 1870s the beach clothing described by *The Housewife* in 1896 as being suitable for a girl is quite enlightened:

'Next to the skin the child should wear a thin woollen gauze combination, very short in the leg: over that a stay body to which is
buttoned a pair of blue serge knickerbockers, unlined. Over that
only one skirt is worn and that should have seven flat buttons
sewn on the wrong side near the hem. On the upper part of the
skirt should be sewn seven corresponding loops, so that for
paddling the desired shortness is easily attained by buttoning the
bottom of the dress to the loops. A little blouse of white serge or
washing silk is worn with the skirt, and a short blue serge jacket
added according to the weather or time of day. Long merino

32. *Even more practical clothes for children were possible when knitted garments became
fashionable. These little girls, dressed in short pleated skirts, knitted fisherman's style
jerseys, swathed sashes, long stockings and knitted brewers' caps, were probably more
comfortable in their clothes on an English beach than children before them. While their
clothes may have been warm in a hot sun, they at least gave the girls a freedom of movement
hitherto unknown. Their brother wears a sailor suit with long trousers.*

33. *Another little boy in a sailor suit, this time in the 1890s. His suit is probably made of serge and has elastic around the bottom of the blouse/jacket, which also has neat buttoning cuffs. The sailor collar with its three lines of white braid may be on a separate shirt worn below the jacket, but even so the jacket has a collar of the same shape. His trousers and his stockings both cover his knees but, like the other boys in sailor suits, he wears a plain round straw hat with a ribbon hanging at the back.*

stockings should be worn; these should pass up under the knickers. To take off the effect of the sun's rays on the head it is as well to give the hat a complete green head lining, using a dull green to avoid arsenical dyes.'

Not all mothers followed this advice. Photographs of girls paddling in the 1890s show many holding up not only skirts but also frilly petticoats.

Boys who did not wear sailor suits, fisherman's jerseys or blazers appeared on the beach in short (knee-length) trousered suits of adult cut, including waistcoats. Tiny children wore bloomers or waders over their ordinary clothes for paddling.

34 (opposite, above). *Children paddling at Great Yarmouth in the 1890s. The taller girl is wearing a yoked dress with a sash and has rolled her skirt up and tied it in a knot at the back. She is wearing short drawers. The girl in a striped dress with a dark sailor collar has tucked her skirt into striped paddlers. The girl on the right has rolled her overall, skirt and petticoat round her waist, revealing short bloomers. She wears a round peaked cap. The other children are wearing straw hats.*

35 (opposite, below). *Children shrimping in a rock pool at Hastings in the early 1890s; note the dark suits worn by the two older boys in the background, the sailor suit worn by the boy on the rocks and the knee-length trousers worn with a dark jacket and straw hat by the boy in the pool. His little sister, who seems to have got very wet, is wearing knee-length drawers, an overall and a white sun-bonnet.*

36 (below). *George Woods was a skilled amateur photographer who, in photographing his wife, his daughter and her friends against the background and people in and around his house at Hastings, has left a record of seaside life in the 1890s that is unique. The photographer's daughter, Margaret, is here seen paddling with three younger friends. Margaret is in her mid teens, short-sighted enough to need narrow metal-rimmed spectacles. On her head she wears a small-crowned flat straw hat with a spotted ribbon. Her dark blouse is patterned with flowers and cut with fashionable leg-of-mutton sleeves. Her skirt (which was probably serge) is folded up and pinned round her waist showing its glazed cotton lining. Beneath the skirt she wears a striped petticoat and white drawers to just above her knee. Margaret's teenage friend in an identical hat, worn on one side of her head, wears a similar skirt folded and held up so that its lining does not show, a white blouse with a lace yoke and a petticoat of indeterminate colour. The two little girls wear overalls, swathed round their waists, holding up, and hiding, their skirts with the petticoats worn beneath them. Their white drawers have elastic round the lower leg which is pulled up to mid-thigh level. The girl on the left wears a peaked round cap, while the youngest child is, unusually, bare-headed.*

37 (above). *Adult paddlers at Hastings c.1890. The dress worn by the woman is very fashionable for that date. She wears a small round cap of a type which today is normally associated with schoolboys but was also popular with women and girls in the late nineteenth century. (See also plates 34 and 36.)*

38 (below left). *Three teenage girls, paddling on the beach at Hastings in the 1890s. They have hitched their skirts up enough to reveal knee-length drawers. The girl on the left has rolled her drawers up to mid thigh and has thrown the back of her skirt over her shoulders like a cape. She wears a wide black shaped belt on a light-coloured dress. All three girls wear tight-fitting dresses that are probably ankle-length. Any fullness in the skirts is gathered or pleated at the back. Their sleeves are leg-of-mutton shaped and they wear medium-brimmed hats decorated with flowers and ribbon.*

39 (below right). *Girls dressing after paddling on the beach at Hastings in the late 1890s. These girls are probably sisters, dressed in white dresses and hats. The girl on the left has her drawers rolled up and her dress tucked into a pair of striped paddling bloomers.*

40. *Photograph by George Woods showing his wife and daughter and a friend with a young daughter on the pier at Hastings. Margaret wears a white blouse, dark skirt and stockings, and a hat decorated with ribbon and little flowers. Mrs Woods wears a smart tailored suit and a hat decorated with feathers. The little girl wears a dress with tucks at the hem; it hangs free from a yoke and has no waistline. She also wears a frilled white hat, tied under her chin with a ribbon, lace-up shoes and white socks. Her mother wears a dark dress patterned with flowers and a dark hat with a feather.*

41. *Toffee-apples for sale from a hand-barrow in Denmark Place, Hastings; they were always popular with children, and the children seen here are probably day visitors, the younger boys in sailor suits, the older ones in dark jackets and small caps. The little girls' hats seem incongruously adult for the size of the wearers. The smaller girl is wearing a cape, the older one a fitted coat. The date is in the mid 1890s.*

42 (above left). *A little girl, dressed after her bathe from one of the bathing-machines seen in the distance, stands on the beach in a dark blue dress or overall with a big frilled collar edged with white. Her slightly floppy sunhat is also white and she wears ankle-strap shoes. She is holding a string that runs out to sea. It could be a fishing line or, more probably, have a boat on the end of it.*

43 (above right). *A little girl on the beach at Skegness in the mid 1890s. The girl in the background is possibly her sister, for they are dressed alike in dark serge dresses with large white collars, black stockings and straw hats trimmed with ribbon. This picture is a detail from a lantern slide.*

44 (below). *Two toddlers on the beach at Blackpool about 1897. They both wear white dresses and large sun-bonnets. The girl on the left has both her dress and her petticoat rolled up round her waist, revealing knee-length drawers, while the child on the right has her dress rolled up but her petticoat is still hanging down. This picture is from a stereoscope pair in the same series as plate 5. It is entitled 'New Women, Blackpool'.*

45. *By the end of the nineteenth century even royalty were taking their own photographs. This picture, taken in 1899 by Alexandra, Princess of Wales (who three years later became Queen Alexandra), shows her son George, Duke of York (later George V), with his children, Prince Albert (later George VI), Prince Edward (later Edward VIII), and Princess Mary, on board the Royal Yacht at Cowes. The two boys wear white sailor suits identical to those worn by thousands of other small boys at this time. Princess Mary wears a white dress and coat, lavishly trimmed with lace, and a straw hat, also trimmed with lace, tying under her chin. While its fabric may be of superior quality, the cut and style of her clothes are the same as the clothes of many other little girls at seaside holidays at this time. The Duke wears light-coloured or white trousers and matching waistcoat, a plain dark blazer and a white yachting cap.*

Greetings from Southsea.

P.V BRADSHAW

The sort of thing
one meets here

I'M HAVING THE TIME OF MY
LIFE AT BLACKPOOL.

"IF I HAD ANOTHER SIXPENCE I'D STOP ANOTHER WEEK."

46 (above left). *A seaside postcard of 1909 showing the clothes of the Edwardian 'masher' in a colourful caricature. All the components of this character's clothes could be seen at the seaside, including the high collar and cravat or necktie with its large tie-pin.*

47 (above right). *A coloured Blackpool postcard posted in 1915. It shows, in cartoon style, the basic holiday clothes of just before the First World War, including the man's boater hat and bow tie, and the plain undecorated hat worn by the woman.*

48 (below). *One of the early postcards used for a portrait photograph. The back is divided into two sections and the left-hand one is headed 'For inland postage only, this space may now be used for communication'. The postage was one halfpenny. The photographer, at Southend, has set up a fake car against a painted promenade and beach background and has photographed this family in their holiday finery. Father is in a dark lounge-suit, Mother in her white dress with a coloured collar, their son in dark trousers and a striped sailor blouse with a coloured collar edged with white braid. The date is 1913.*

5. Holidaymakers' clothes 1900-20

The seaside postcard

The first postcards appeared in Britain in 1870 but they did not take their present form until 1902, when the Post Office permitted cards, with a picture on one side and a message and an address on the other, to be sent through the post. From this date onwards postcards were produced and used by the million, not only in Britain but all over the world.

The greatest number, and the most popular, were topographical photographs of views, with or without people in them. Some of the photographs in the latter part of this book had their origins as picture postcards. But postcards were produced in many media and on every subject, including bathing belles, beach scenes and the comic seaside cartoons, in which large active women and small put-upon men fought the continuing battle of the sexes in a variety of seaside situations.

Both the photographs and the cartoons reproduced on postcards show the people on them in contemporary clothes, although the cartoons were often simplified. Beach photographers of the first decade of the twentieth century onwards usually produced their pictures as postcards, and the popularity of the postcard brought the end of the Victorian carte-de-visite.

Some beach photographers had life-size postcards pasted on to boards with holes where the heads of the characters would have been, so that their clients could stand behind the boards with their heads through the holes, to be photographed dressed as the characters in the cartoons; others had model trains, and later cars, in which their clients could sit and be photographed.

Postcards were collected as enthusiastically as they were posted; postcard albums were produced for them, and in the specialised antiques field of the late twentieth century some of the early twentieth-century postcards can fetch extremely high prices.

Apart from any monetary value, a collection of seaside postcards, both photographic and drawn, can give a student of costume and fashion a great deal of useful information, but it should be remembered that any one photograph produced as a postcard probably sold over a period of five years. The postmark is a guide to the average date the clothes in the picture were worn, not the earliest or latest.

49. *Bathing-machines, tipped at an uncomfortable angle, about 1905. The children on the beach are watching other children and adults in the water. The boy in the centre of the picture is wearing the top of his sailor suit over his swimming costume, which has shorter than normal legs.*

Beach and bathing costumes, 1900-20

From the time that sea-bathing began in the British Isles the men and women bathers had been very strictly segregated. The same rules did not apply in Europe. After 1871 some middle-class families went to France or Belgium, where, in places like Dieppe, Boulogne or Ostend, mixed bathing was allowed and families could sit on the beach in their bathing-costumes, playing with their children. By 1900 many people had come to feel that this should be allowed in Britain too. One of the first resorts to permit mixed bathing was Bexhill, East Sussex, in 1901. Bexhill had always prided itself on its family atmosphere, and mixed bathing was introduced with the aim of attracting families with younger children to the town. By 1914 mixed bathing was almost universal, only a few resorts retaining periods of segregated swimming for those who preferred it. Once people were allowed to sit or play on the beach in bathing-costumes, it became extremely difficult to prevent them from undressing on the beach. Bathing-machines were gradually abandoned in favour of beach huts or tents.

56. *Mrs Ada Renow and Mrs Mabel McCarthy pose in their bathing-costumes at Margate in 1918. Their costumes and caps are made of cotton stockinette.*

exception to this rule. The fashion writer in *The Sketch* for 14th August 1901 reported: 'I notice that ocean millinery grows to an acute angle of crescendo . . . Bathing caps and hats are objects of the utmost piquancy, and the Creole silk turban of many gay colours is more elaborately fashioned this year than of yore. Smart frilled silk caps, something after the Breton order, are charmingly becoming and, by devices of wily whalebone, remain still and erect even after immersion in Channel waves. Dainty straw hats, wide, trimmed and tied down from both sides with ribbon-strings, are much affected by those who permit the waves to come as far as the neckline but no further. Some women go to the extreme of pinning curls under the brim of their Creole bathing-caps which curl naturally and so preserve the wearers' external picturesqueness even after immersion.' Nobody ever went into the sea or played on the beach bare-headed until just before the First World War, when a few bare heads began to be seen.

The American fashion of wearing stockings with bathing-costumes came to British beaches for a few years at the beginning of the twentieth century but by 1910 had disappeared. On sandy beaches women were bare-legged and bare-footed again, but on pebbly beaches shoes of some kind had always been worn.

Once people began to stay on the beach in bathing-costumes a new garment came into general use. This was the beach wrap, a cape or cloak-like garment made of towelling or even of a water-proof fabric lined with towelling or a fancy fabric. The same fashion writer in *The Sketch* of 1901 who described the bathing caps also described bathing wraps, giving them the name of *peignoir* (since they originated in France): 'Superseding the old Turkey towelling *peignoir* which was monotonously white and shapeless in outline, we now have daintily made substitutes in pink, blue, mauve or green flannel, serge or blanketing, flanked with big Capuchin hoods and wide collars.'

Beachwear and promenade clothes: men

Blazers and boater hats continued as popular seaside wear for men, although these were now worn with white or grey trousers rather than dark ones. Waistcoats were never worn with blazers, although they continued to be part of a lounge-suit. When jackets were taken off on the beach long shirt sleeves were visible; collars and ties were still worn on a beach as part of 'normal' dress. Flannel trousers and Norfolk-style jackets were increasingly used as leisure wear by young men. Tweed or flannel 'sports' jackets were also beginning to make an appearance. Some men wore summer jackets of cream alpaca over dark trousers and waist-coats. Panama straw hats, lighter in weight and softer than a boater, were beginning to be popular and were gradually to oust the boater.

The First World War put an end to some seaside activities along the south and east coast, where the seaside piers became embarkation points for troops going to France. Elsewhere on the coast of the British Isles there was little change and seaside life seemed to go on as before the war, although at a quieter and slower pace, the only outward difference being men on leave in uniform. Those men who did not join the forces continued to wear the clothes that were fashionable in 1914.

Beachwear and promenade costume: women

The Edwardian period is notable in dress history for the intro-duction of the S-shaped corset that gave the impression that the

57. *Royalty on the beach at Seaford, East Sussex, in 1905. This photograph was taken by Queen Alexandra's daughter, Princess Victoria, of her cousin Constantine, Duke of Sparta, later Constantine I of Greece, his wife, Sophie, Duchess of Sparta, and their younger daughter, Princess Irene of Greece, during a holiday visit to England. The little princess is wearing a large frilled white bonnet and a white dress with a big collar. She appears to have a striped towel tied round her over her skirt and her white drawers show beneath it. The Duke wears a dark suit and a panama hat while the Duchess wears a skirt and jacket in a pale striped fabric, a lace-trimmed blouse and a straw hat with a dark ribbon and a spotted veil.*

58. *Three women riding seaside donkeys somewhere on the north-east coast about 1909. Their summer dresses have three-quarter-length sleeves. Two of them have elaborately folded and tucked bodices and tight wide belts. The woman on the right wears a plainer dress of striped fabric with a deep neckline filled in with a blouse with a high collar. The stripes of the fabric are used as a decoration round the low neck of the dress, and the skirt is trimmed with four deep tucks. Their hats are large, perched on padded bouffant hair styles.*

top half of the body of a woman wearing it was one step ahead of her lower half. The S-shaped corset, with the high boned collars of the women's dresses or blouses, made a fashionable woman appear a very stiff and inflexible figure. When the S-shaped corset went out of fashion and lighter, simpler clothes came into fashion in 1912, the seaside was the ideal place to show them off. The extreme of fashion, the hobble skirt, may have appeared at Ascot, but probably few of them were seen at the seaside. The photographs of women in clothes other than bathing-costumes show that easy-fitting practical clothes in the form of skirts and blouses predominated at the seaside in the years 1911 to 1914. It was these practical clothes that were worn during the First World War, the skirts rising in 1915 almost to mid calf, and dropping again slowly by 1918 to just above the ankle.

Beachwear and promenade costume: children

In the Edwardian period children wore similar clothes to those of the 1890s. Sailor suits for boys and girls were still popular,

59. *A family group in 1911. The generations can be distinguished by their clothes, the oldest woman wearing a large hat and an elaborate blouse and bolero, the younger women in simpler-styled clothes. However, all the men wear jackets, collars and ties. Note the changing tent and the deck-chairs stacked in the background. Deck-chairs as we know them first appeared on beaches for hire in the late 1890s. This type of deck-chair was first known as a hammock chair and they were originally made as camp furniture for the army in India in the 1870s. Later they were used on board ship — hence the name 'deck-chair' — and finally became common on British beaches.*

60 (left). *This young couple visited Great Yarmouth in 1913 and had their photograph taken at the studio of Walter Kelf in Regent Road. These are the clothes they would have worn on the promenade. Her dress was plain and white, with a sailor collar and a small brooch at the neck. Her hat was a crocheted white 'Juliet' cap, a fashionable alternative to a wide-brimmed straw hat. He wears a dark three-piece suit with a watch chain and fancy fob on his waistcoat. His hat is a straw boater with a plain wide ribbon.*

61 (right). *Two girls on holiday in Southsea pose for their portrait in Berkshire Bros, a photographic studio, in 1912 or 1913. Their dresses show the new outline that was popular just before the First World War. The skirts are straight and fairly narrow, and the necklines low in comparison to the very high necks of Edwardian dresses. The cut of the bodices is simple in comparison to the draped, tucked and ruched bodices of the previous decade. One girl wears a lace overskirt and her frilled dress bodice fastens diagonally to her left hip; the other girl's dress is laced down the left front and she has a sailor collar. Both girls wear wide belts. There was a great deal of experimentation in dress designs between 1911 and 1914, which sometimes produced very unusual effects.*

although little girls were equally likely to wear white frilled dresses and elaborate sun-bonnets. Boys' sailor suits were often white, whereas in the 1890s they had been dark blue.

When not wearing sailor suits, boys wore knickerbocker trousers, shirts and jackets or blazers. Waistcoats for boys began to disappear and some Edwardian photographs show boys at the seaside in knickerbockers, held up with belts, and white shirts with dark-coloured short ties. Even children wore hats at the seaside — the boys flat caps, straw hats or even bowlers, the girls straw hats or sun-bonnets — and both boys and girls wore long

62. One of the younger members of the Ely family in 1906 wears a striped dress tucked into baggy bloomers. She wears a knitted brewer's cap with a tassel.

63 (right). *A slightly joky postcard carrying a photograph of a plump little girl in waders. The original photograph was taken at Brighton about 1912 or 1913.*

64 (left). *Two children and their grand-mother on the beach at Keyhaven, Hamp-shire, in 1918. The little boy is wearing bathing trunks (hidden by the towel) while his sister is wearing her petticoat as a sun dress. Their grandmother is much more formally dressed in dark skirt and striped blouse decorated with tucks and braid. She wears an old-fashioned 'habit shirt' (an under-blouse, usually consisting of a collar with a yoke which ties at the sides under the arms) to fill in the neckline of her blouse.*

black stockings when not paddling in the sea.

Toddlers' bloomers or waders were now made of a waterproof material and were bright scarlet or yellow. Some were horizon-tally striped in these colours, some had bib fronts. They kept splashes off the child's clothes and enabled the child to be easily seen. They were more often used for girls than boys, but a few very small boys wore them.

65. *When the Yarmouth councillors were planning the grand opening of their new open-
air beach swimming-pool in 1922, the Mayor, Councillor F. Brett, challenged the chairman
of the Beach Committee, Alderman W. H. Bayfield, to a swimming race of 35 yards (32
metres). The challenge was accepted and, after formally declaring the pool open, they met,
both clad in bathing-costumes, on the edge of the pool. The race was featured in all the
local newspapers along with enthusiastic descriptions of the delights and facilities in the new
pool. Both men were over fifty but had been keen swimmers all their lives. Their costumes
were regulation style, although younger men would have shortened the legs a little. The
Mayor, using a powerful side stroke, won the race, to the delight of the crowd.*

6. Holidaymakers' clothes 1920-39

After the First World War the world never quite returned to the formality that had existed in 1913. The younger generation was determined to exercise a right of choice in all things and what they chose with regard to holiday clothes was the cult of the sun; for the first time in history it became fashionable to expose the body to the sun and to flaunt both it and a tanned skin.

Bathing-costumes: men

The bathing-costumes of the 1920s for both men and women showed, almost year by year, an increase in the amount of skin exposed and a decrease in the weight and amount of fabric used. The horizontally striped costume with legs and sleeves disappeared, laughed out of existence as old-fashioned. While many men wore bathing-costumes that covered their torso, these costumes had low necks and backs, with fabric no wider than straps holding them over the shoulders, and legs that were no longer than an inch or two. These costumes were nearly always made in plain dark colours — black, navy, maroon or royal blue. As the decade progressed the top half of these costumes at first was made in a different, lighter colour, then became more and more cut away and finally disappeared altogether. Young men in the 1930s bathed in swimming trunks differing from later fashions only in that they usually covered the navel and often had belts around the waist. Even the legs of such trunks disappeared in favour of a line that went horizontally across the body at the level of the groin in front and just below the buttocks at the back.

Bathing-costumes for men and women had begun to be made in stockinette from the end of the first decade of the twentieth century. In the 1920s the newest fabric was machine-knitted wool. By the 1930s men's bathing-costumes were always of wool and cotton stockinette was no longer used. By the 1930s, too, most men owned a bathing-costume or a pair of swimming trunks. While many swimming-pools still hired out costumes, the disappearance of the bathing-machines largely removed the facility of hiring a swimming costume from the beaches. However, these changes came about gradually, the younger people and more go-ahead resorts adopting them first. Even in the late 1930s it was still possible to find men wearing bathing-costumes with short legs and sleeves, while in the quieter old-fashioned seaside towns a swimming costume could still be hired on the beach.

66 (above). *Three children bathing in the mid 1920s. The boy on the left and the girl, centre, are wearing identical bathing-costumes of cotton stockinette. The girl on the right is wearing a striped costume that could be made of wool. Her cap is a rubberised mob-cap.*

67 (left). *Harry Jennings with his daughter, Patricia, at Woolacombe Sands, Devon, in August 1934. He wears bathing trunks with short legs, while two-year-old Patricia wears white rompers and a cardigan.*

Bathing-costumes: women

Women's bathing-costumes in the early 1920s could still be one-piece or two-piece, made either as a combination costume or as knickers and tunic. Like the man's costumes they shrank, firstly in the sleeves, then in the length of leg.

The fashion writer in *The Tatler* on 17th May 1922 describes a combination costume made in silk stockinette for the serious swimmer as a 'swimming suit'. It had legs to mid thigh, a wide belt, but no sleeves, only shoulder-straps. Draped silk turbans were recommended wear on the head with these one-piece costumes.

The two-piece costumes were much more elaborate. They usually had dark knickers with mid-thigh-length legs and a sleeveless tunic reaching to just below the buttocks. These tunics were often no more than a tabard-shaped length of cloth, brightly patterned,

68 (left). *A group of bathing belles on the steps of a changing cabin at Bournemouth in 1920. They show the variety of headgear worn for swimming at this time.*

69 (right). *Rubber slip-on beach shoes of the mid 1920s. They were usually made in two colours with the sole only slightly thicker than the upper. Note the colourful sunshades to keep off the sun and the bangles worn by the girl on the right.*

70. *Miss Ivy Hawke, who swam the Channel on 18th and 19th August 1923, in a two-piece bathing-costume consisting of very short drawers and thigh-length tunic trimmed with white braid.*

71 (left). *Two girls in very fashionable bathing-costumes in 1929. Both costumes were made of machine-knitted wool and were probably quite brightly coloured. The white belts on bathing-costumes were fashionable from about 1927 to about 1931 or 1932.*

72 (right). *Mother and daughter at Weston-super-Mare in 1932. The mother, Mrs Dorothy Anderson, is the toddler Dorothy Wood shown on the title page. Here she wears a parti-coloured bathing-costume with a belt, while her eleven-year-old daughter Bette wears a plain dark bathing-costume, also with a white belt. Bette is shown as a toddler in plate 91.*

with a hole for the head. They tied at the waist each side. While some women did swim in them, they were perhaps meant more for playing on the beach, for they were made in fabrics that could range from cotton to silk, satin or taffeta. Serious swimmers who wanted a two-piece costume chose a stockinette-type fabric made up as knickers and a thigh-length close-fitting tunic.

By the late 1920s the backs of the one-piece costumes were lower than the fronts and the two-piece tunic costume had disappeared. In the 1930s costumes were normally of wool stockinette and large parts of their fabric were cut away. The backs became very low indeed, right down to the waist or slightly below

73 (left). *Two little girls on the steps of a beach hut at Lowestoft in 1934. These two-year-olds wore white sun-bonnets patterned in blue. The girl on the left had a plain blue bathing-costume; the one on the right had a costume that was pale blue at the bottom and pale yellow at the top with a little duckling appliquéd on one side. Both costumes were made of knitted wool and both little girls had slip-on rubber beach shoes, one blue and white, the other yellow and white.*

74 (below left). *Three-year-old Patricia Jennings, at Ferring, West Sussex, in 1935, wears a cut-away wool bathing costume and a white sun-bonnet.*

75 (below right). *In 1933 the first juvenile sea angling competition was held on St Leonards-on-Sea pier. This young competitor wore a white swimming costume and beret in which to take part. She was about nine or ten years old. The girl behind her wore shorts and a striped singlet.*

76. *A photograph taken on the pier at Llandudno on 27th June 1935 shows very clearly the cut of three 1930s bathing costumes. They would all have been made of knitted wool. The striped costume on the left would have had a 'halter' fastening at the back of the neck (hidden here by the brim of the wearer's hat). It may well have had a panel of fabric at the front joining the two parts. The centre costume has large circles cut out of the sides, while the one on the right has a very low-cut back. All three costumes have minimal legs and come below the buttocks. The woven straw hats were sold at the seaside in their thousands. Sometimes the hats were made of folded paper strips woven or plaited together. Most of them were imported, being made in Japan or Hong Kong for export to Europe. The three girls, who are possibly professional models, wear the high-heeled court shoes that were considered glamorous in the 1930s. The picture may have been taken to advertise the 'penny-in-the-slot' machines on the pier, or as an advertisement for holidays in Llandudno.*

— sometimes so low that the shoulder-straps were crossed over the back to button at the lower sides, in order to keep them on. Sometimes the sides of the costumes were cut away, leaving a narrow panel up the centre of the back. In some cases so much was cut from the sides that the costume almost became a two-piece, consisting of waist-high trunks very similar to those worn by men and a brassiere top to cover the breasts, leaving a bare midriff in front. The two were joined at the sides and back of the neck, like a halter. Sometimes the costume was one-piece in front but appeared from the back to be separate trunks and top. Very occasionally, by the end of the 1930s the costume did consist of

77. *Two teenage girls on the beach near Dawlish Cove, Devon, about 1933. Their wool bathing-costumes were very fashionable. The girl on the left has a corselet shape knitted into the front of her costume and a knitted belt made of the same wool. The girl on the right has a white wool costume with a thick twisted-colour cord as a belt and as shoulder straps. Both costumes have the vestigial skirt across the front of the lower part of the costume.*

78. *The 'cult of the sun' strikingly portrayed in a plain regulation bathing-costume of 1930.*

79 (left). *Percy Cladish, a young man in his early twenties, with a friend on the beach at Lowestoft in 1931, wraps himself in a beach towel of brilliant orange and yellow on a dark background. The 'rising sun' design was a popular motif in the 1930s.*

80 (right). *Biddy Wilson, aged eleven, wears a striped beach towel made into a wrap in 1930. Both this and the wrap in plate 79 were made by sewing a tape along one side of the towel a little way in from the edge, and passing a draw-string through the channel, so forming a cloak with a collar.*

separate trunks and brassiere. Then the two parts were quite substantial: the trunks always covered the navel and the top covered all the breasts.

Although the knickers and long-tunic costume disappeared in the late 1920s the lower edge of this tunic survived into the 1930s as a vestigial skirt on the front part of women's swimming costumes, giving a straight horizontal line at groin level. By the end of the 1930s a new elasticated fabric called Lastex was being used for swimming costumes.

Some swimmers wore plain rubber bathing caps designed to keep the hair dry. These caps became commonplace on all beaches by the end of the 1920s, ousting the fancy turbans and frilled caps of the earlier part of the century. In the 1930s no other style of bathing cap than plain rubber was seen, usually white.

Bathing shoes, like the bathing cap, became slip-on covers of plain rubber in the 1930s. They could be any colour, including black or white, and were usually worn only on pebbly beaches as protection to the feet.

Far more attention was paid to the bathing wrap or cape. These were of towelling or of shantung lined with fine towelling. Large coloured and patterned towels could double as a towel or a wrap. Some of these larger towels, with a draw-string along one longer edge, could be used as a cloak or screen under which to undress or dress.

Beach and promenade wear: men

As acquiring a suntan became more popular, many new garments came on to the market for sports and leisure wear and these were worn on beaches before or after swimming. White flannel trousers, held up by belts, and open-neck shirts became commonplace among younger men. By the 1930s shirt sleeves were as acceptable on the pier as on the beach. Blazers and sports jackets were worn for warmth when needed. In place of a waistcoat a 'Fair Isle', brightly patterned sleeveless knitted pullover could be worn over an open-neck shirt. Older men continued to wear braces, waistcoats, collars and ties even at the seaside. Their concession to the holiday spirit was the wearing of white or fawn alpaca or linen jackets in place of the dark suit jacket that was their normal wear.

It has been said before of men's wear that one generation's leisure clothes become the formal clothes of their grandsons. In the 1880s the lounge-suit was strictly leisure wear for the middle

81. A game on the putting green at Cliftonville, Kent, in 1923. The younger woman wears a fashionable pleated skirt, jacket and cloche hat, the older woman a more old-fashioned brimmed hat with a very fashionable side-fastening coat. Note the length of the schoolboy's shorts.

and upper classes. By the 1930s it had become work wear for the lower middle class and formal wear for the working class. Leisure wear for the middle class could be a blazer or, further down the social scale, a sports jacket worn over grey flannel trousers. In the mid 1920s there was a vogue (starting among undergraduates) for very wide-legged trousers known as 'Oxford bags'. By the 1930s a more popular garment was a pair of 'plus-fours', the very baggy knickerbockers with a buttoned band at the knee, over which the fabric drooped to mid calf, which had been invented for golfing wear before the First World War. They were regarded at first as strictly functional sportswear for golfers only but in the 1930s were often worn on seaside holidays by men who never played golf but liked the plus-fours for their comfort and difference from normal working gear. Young men could wear shorts instead of trousers for cycling, camping, playing tennis or on the beach. These shorts usually ended just above the knee. Shirt sleeves were worn rolled up in warm weather and short-sleeved shirts came on the market.

Many young men abandoned hats at the seaside as the 1920s progressed. The boater had disappeared by 1930 and panama hats were worn on beaches only by middle-aged or older men.

82. *Mr and Mrs Smith on the cliff top at Cliftonville in 1925 or 1926. He wears a sports jacket and grey flannel trousers. Her striped dress and cloche hat are very typical of the mid 1920s, as is her long necklace.*

Beach and promenade wear: women

During the 1920s a new costume for young women appeared on beaches. This was the 'beach pyjama' suit, consisting of long trousers and a jacket, that could be worn over a swimming costume or knickers and blouse. The beach pyjamas were made of lightweight fabrics such as silk stockinette in vivid colours edged with black, bright floral or geometrically patterned cottons or linens. They had elastic or draw-string waists and the jackets were normally 'edge to edge' with no fastenings.

These beach pyjamas of the mid 1920s gave way to the slacks of the 1930s — wide straight-legged or bell-bottomed trousers made of woollen or heavy linen fabric. These trousers for women fastened with a placket on the left hip. They could be closed by buttons or press-studs but never fastened down the front like men's trousers; even when made by a man's tailor they fastened down the side.

By 1939 cotton dungarees worn over short-sleeved blouses were also fashionable for beach wear, as were 'play suits' with above-the-knee skirts. These play suits were sometimes made with backless halter-necked bodices with matching coatees or boleros, or as very short button-through dresses worn over

83. *On the promenade, about 1929. The woman wears a white skirt with a centre pleat and a 'jumper-blouse' of fabric with a crocheted waistband. She wears white shoes and stockings and a bandeau round her hair. The man wears white flannel trousers with turn-ups, white shoes and socks, an open-necked shirt, a cricketing pullover with the club's colours at the vee-neck, and a white blazer with a badge on the pocket.*

84. *Relaxing after her swim at Woolacombe, Devon, in 1937, blonde-haired Dell chooses a white linen blouse and pleated shorts, worn with a dark scarf spotted with white.*

85. *Three young women paddling in a rock pool at Eastbourne in 1921. They wear cotton dresses to mid calf or just below the knee and long knitted jackets. Their hats have deep crowns and medium-wide brims.*

86. *Four teenage girls on the beach at one of the large resorts on the north-east coast in 1927. They wear knee-length white dresses and white stockings and shoes, with long jackets or cardigans over their dresses. The girl on the left has a sleeveless cardigan with a belt. The north-east coast is often very windy and the girls' hair is blown about by the wind. Two of the girls wear fashionable wide bandeaus over their foreheads to hold their hair in place.*

matching shorts and unbuttoned from the waist down. Shorts and blouses were also worn on the beach.

Other women wore their everyday cotton dresses under knitted jackets in the 1920s and waist-length cardigans in the 1930s. Hats were still common on the beaches in the 1920s, made in floral cottons or plain linen. Panama hats were worn by women in the early 1930s, but head scarves or no head covering at all were more common by the end of the decade. Shoes for the beach varied from the rubber slip-ons worn in the water to plimsolls; sandals varied from an almost solid leather shoe style with punched cut-out patterns across the toe portion to rope-soled espadrilles held on with tape or ribbon lacing round the ankle.

In dull, windy or cold weather people still walked on the beach, and coats, mackintoshes, hats and head scarves became holiday wear. Jumpers and pullovers were practical fashionable garments and these, too, would have been worn on the beach on cooler days.

87 (left). *Mrs Kathleen Farrow in a buttercup-yellow linen dress, white beret, beads and tan-and-white shoes, on the steps of a beach hut at Lowestoft in 1935.*

88 (right). *A Dawlish housewife, Mrs Vince, relaxes with her dog at the family beach hut at Coryton Cove, Devon, in August 1938. Beach huts were usually hired in the larger resorts, but in small seaside villages and quiet coves they could be the private property of a family who would then loan it, or occasionally hire it, to their friends or relations. The picture shows the very small dimensions of a beach hut, and the type of furnishing that was usual. Mrs Vince wears a plain cotton dress, a woollen cardigan and sandals for her day on the beach.*

Beach and promenade clothes: children

The notable difference between the photographs of children in the early 1900s and those taken in the 1920s is in the amount of clothes they wore. Small boys' knee-length trousers became shorts, above the knee in the early 1920s and shorter still in the 1930s. The younger the boy, the shorter his shorts. Waistcoats for boys vanished, pullovers taking their place. Short sleeves became

89 (above). *A family group in 1920 somewhere on the south coast. Note the broderie anglaise on the girls' white dresses. White was a very popular colour for children's and women's clothes in the three years following the First World War. Striped cotton summer dresses were very fashionable in the early to mid 1920s, and Mrs Ada Renow, seated left, has a very up-to-the-minute dress in a striped fabric with a white collar and a darker bow. She is the woman in the swimming costume (left) in plate 56. The older man (centre) is still wearing a boater. By the mid 1920s they were right out of fashion.*

90 and 91 (opposite, above). *Little Doreen Slatter at Bognor Regis in 1924 (left) and little Bette Anderson at Weston-super-Mare in 1925 (right). Both wear rubber waders into which their dresses were tucked while paddling or making sand-castles on the beach.*

92 (right). *Two boys on the beach at Southport on holiday during the Lancashire wakes week in August 1927. James and Harry Fenton, five and four years old, wear new sage-green linen suits made by their mother and baker-boy tweed caps made by their grandmother. They build sand-castles with colourful new tin buckets and spades.*

93 (far right). *A two-year-old boy photographed in 1931 on a beach groyne. His beach play suit is made of cotton sateen in two colours and he wears white sandals.*

94. *Paul Spriggs, in his second year, on the beach in 1932. His play suit is made of pale blue wool and was knitted by his mother. It is a one-piece combination garment with a separate belt. He also wears white sandals.*

95. *Mr Parker with his young son on the beach at Seaton in 1931 or 1932, showing that the sailor suit for little boys remained in fashion for a period of about eighty years. The only difference between this little boy and the others pictured in sailor suits in this book is the length of the shorts. Like those of the little princes in plate 45, this boy's sailor suit is white.*

commonplace. Hats were still worn in the 1920s, linen and cotton hats for little boys, 'baker-boy caps' for slightly older ones. Once he had started school, the schoolboy's close-fitting cap was a boy's normal wear even on a beach, except that when wearing a swimming costume he was bare-headed.

By the 1930s sun-tanned children played on beaches in minimal woollen swimming costumes or cotton play suits. These consisted of short shorts and short-sleeved shirts for boys, and short

96. *Two girls aged four and five at Lowestoft in 1935 or 1936. Over a dark bathing-costume in machine-knitted wool one little girl wears an embroidered bolero. The older girl wears a plain cotton or linen dress. It could have been pale blue, pale green or yellow, all popular colours for children's clothes at this time. Both little girls wear white sandals and large white bows in their short hair.*

skirts with bib fronts and straps crossing over the back for little girls. Some still wore hats, especially in the early 1930s, but hats became less common towards the end of the decade. Health and comfort, rather than fashion, dictated what children wore on the beach. On the promenade little girls wore jackets over their sun suits, or they wore short-sleeved short-skirted dresses made of bright cotton fabrics.

7. Residents and workers at the seaside

Most seaside resorts were originally small fishing villages or towns. Their business and livelihood depended on the sea as a source of food or trade. Some of the smaller villages wrested their living from the land as well as the sea, their inhabitants being both farmers and fishermen, working at either trade according to the season. This chapter looks at some of these seaside residents who wore the everyday dress of their class and time without concerning themselves with holiday fashions.

Fishermen and their families

Fishermen of the 1860s wore knitted caps on their heads and knitted upper garments, known as jerseys, guernseys or ganzies, which originated on the islands around Britain, where native sheep's wool was made into these garments by the womenfolk of the district. There is a tradition that the sometimes quite elaborate cable stitches knitted into these fishermen's jerseys varied from village to village, so that the body of a drowned fisherman could be identified — at least as to where he came from — when washed ashore. The fisherman's jersey was usually dark blue. It took the place of a jacket and was worn over a grey or blue collarless shirt and dark blue trousers. At work on the beach they wore on top of these clothes a short canvas smock (sometimes called a slop). In Hastings, East Sussex, the fishermen's smocks were hung up to dry in the tan house and became smoked to a rich brown colour. These smocks protected their clothes from the fish and the dirt of the lines and nets. At sea they wore other canvas smocks, impregnated in the eighteenth century by black tar, and in the nineteenth century by boiled linseed oil and pipeclay, giving a yellow colour. Their sea-going hats were sou'westers, with a wider brim at the back than the front, which prevented water from going down the backs of their smocks. These clothes do not seem to have varied in style between 1850 and the years just before the First World War. Ashore they took off their smocks, revealing the jersey and, by 1890, wore hats that could vary from a soft round cap with a small peak or a harder, higher, peaked cap to a bowler hat or occasionally a black beret in the south of England and a Tam o' Shanter in the north. Black or dark blue jackets seem to have been worn only by the elderly fishermen, and then only on shore.

The wives and daughters of fishermen wore plain dresses over mid-calf-length petticoats. When they were gathering bait,

97 (above left). *A daguerreotype photograph by Joseph Chadwick Peatson showing two shrimpers of the late 1850s or early 1860s. It is a picture posed for pictorial effect rather than a photograph of men at work, but it shows their nets and the baskets used for collecting the shrimps and inshore fish and lobsters as well as their clothing and boots. One man is wearing a short smock (also known as a slop or a frock in various parts of Britain) and a battered hat that may be a form of sou'wester with a longer brim at the back. The older, seated man is wearing an oilskin jacket over a short smock and dark trousers. The jacket is fastened at the neck only. His hat appears to be a felt hat with an indented crown. Both men have clay pipes. The shrimpers' long wading boots, folded down and turned up again so that they take up less room, are balanced in the bar of the big shrimping net. In wear they would have been pulled up to the thighs.*

98 (above right). *A Hastings fisherman and his daughter in the mid 1890s. The girl wears a white overall on top of a dark skirt and patterned blouse. Unlike the visiting children, who almost always wore hats or caps, she wears a country sun-bonnet.*

99 (left). *Two schoolboy residents of Dawlish who owned their own boat, which they kept on the foreshore among the fishing boats, were photographed in 1937 under the watchful eye of an old fisherman. He wore dark trousers and jacket, a knitted jersey and a flat cap. The boys, sixteen-year-old Philip Daniell and his friend, had gone straight to the boat from school; Philip is wearing his school cap. Neither boy would have specific leisure clothes as we would know them today. Living at the seaside, they scorned the holidaymakers' 'fancy' clothes as pretence and wore the same clothes on the beach or in the boat as they did at school or at home. Taking off their ties on a hot day was the only concession these grammar-school boys made to the summer weather, though on a wet day they wore fisherman's oilskins in their boat, over their ordinary clothes.*

A FIRST PEEP.

100 (left). *The 'old salt', a familiar figure at many a Victorian seaside, was usually a retired sailor who acted as a beach attendant, earning a few pence by carrying chairs, prams or bags along the beach for visitors, giving 'trips round the bay' in his boat, or allowing children to look through his telescope. This old sailor, drawn by John Leech in the 1850s, wears rolled-up trousers, a fisherman's jersey and a top-hat. The child, who may well be a small boy, wears button boots, long drawers and a tartan dress or overall.*

101 (right). *One of the crew of the 'Albertine', a sea-going pleasure yacht that gave trips to visitors to Hastings in the 1890s. The crew wore white duck trousers, fisherman's jerseys printed with the boat's name and peaked caps. The first boat named 'Albertine' was built in 1865 and the trippers were carried on to the boat by the crew who waded through the waves. By the time the second 'Albertine' was built, in 1885, steps and planks helped passengers to disembark. The empty boat was hauled up the beach on wire ropes by a horse capstan, turned round on a turntable, loaded with more passengers, then released into the sea. The boat trips were so popular that a third boat, 'The New Albertine', was built in 1891 and ran until 1924.*

shrimps or cockles on the shore the dresses could be bunched up to make them shorter, or tied at the knee to resemble breeches. As protection for their clothes when baiting lines or gutting fish they wore aprons, but on other occasions the apron could be rolled up and swathed round the waist to be out of the way. Their sleeves were usually long, and oversleeves could be worn as protection.

The womenfolk also had the task of selling the fish and quickly realised that a distinctive, easily recognisable dress was a good

102. *Fisherwomen of Llangwym photographed at Tenby, Dyfed, in the late 1870s or early 1880s. These were the clothes they wore to sell fish, cockles and shrimps to seaside visitors. The women are pictured wearing their 'traditional' ankle-length skirts, with tucks round the hems, plain dark or Paisley-patterned jackets, long aprons of plain linen or checked flannel, flannel or knitted shawls round their shoulders and white scarves or caps round their heads under felt hats. The clothes they wore every day at home would have been similar in cut and style to these before 1850 but were probably shabbier and certainly became plainer towards the end of the century as the women became aware of and were able to afford 'fashionable' dress. The distinctive style of clothes seen in this picture became a costume that was worn by the South Wales fisherwomen and cockle-gatherers to sell their wares well into the twentieth century.*

advertisement, especially when selling to holidaymakers. The Scottish fisherwomen from Aberdeen and Newhaven (near Edinburgh) wore calf-length striped petticoats under a plain dark dress bunched up at the back.

In the north of England fisherwomen wore ankle-length woollen skirts, heavily decorated with horizontal tucks. They

103. *The bathing-machines on the men's beach c.1880, at Freshwater, Isle of Wight, have planks set across the edge of the water to enable the bathers to reach them. The man in waistcoat, shirt, trousers and bowler hat, with a towel over his arm, is probably the proprietor. The people sitting on the beach near him are all men and boys. A boy is walking the plank from the bathing-machine to the beach. The photograph was taken by Russell Sedgefield.*

104. *St Catherine's Rock, Tenby, Dyfed, c.1899. These bathing-machines were drawn by horses into the water. Note the proprietor with two horses on the left of the picture. The advertisements on the side of the machines, as well as the clothes of the ladies on the beach, proclaim this photograph to have been taken around 1900.*

105. *A page from the 'Bexhill Pictorial Guide' for 1894, advertising W. J. Flint's bathing-machines and other beach services. The statement, 'Orders taken for sea water', refers to the practice of delivering sea water in tubs for people to use for cold baths in their lodging houses or hotels. Another advertiser in the same guide states 'Sea water carried'.*

wore small shawls round their shoulders and sometimes tied these shawls round their heads as head scarves. In Wales the fisherwomen wore ankle-length skirts, jackets, checked aprons and shawls, with scarves around their heads under their hats. But these deliberately picturesque clothes were often reserved only for market days and while selling fish to visitors. At home they changed into plainer, poorer clothes with large rough aprons and heavy boots. Sun-bonnets were the finishing touch for women in the south of England, where the fishermen's wives did not do the work of selling the fish.

Landladies and hotel servants

Accommodation for holidaymakers could range, even in 1860, from a rented room in someone else's home to a grand hotel whose uniformed staff gave the impression that the holiday-makers were staying in a stately home with many servants to wait upon them. The room in someone else's house was almost always under the control of the lady of the house, for letting rooms was a means whereby a woman could make extra money.

Although seaside landladies have been the butt of cartoonists and comedians for two hundred years, they gave, and still give, a

106. *At Gorleston, near Great Yarmouth, the Capps' bathing-machines were a familiar sight in the 1890s, ranged in a long row at the edge of the water. There were thirteen single machines and these cost 3d per person a time for their use, which included the use of a towel and bathing-dress by the hirer. Swimming lessons were given by Mr Capps and his sons to those who applied for them. By 1900 there were also at least three family machines which were double width and had two doors at the landward side leading into a vestibule with a single door at the water's edge. The single machines were numbered 1 to 13, the family machines 14 onwards. In this picture the founder of the business, known as Grandfather Capps, stands on the platform of machine number 16, a family machine. On the right of the picture is his son, William Isaac Capps, on the steps his other son, Whitmore Capps, holding the life-buoy, and on the left of the picture an assistant thought to be a Mr Bensley, who subsequently started his own business. William Capps and Mr Bensley are holding the harnesses, attached to ropes and poles which were put on the pupil learning to swim. (The swimming instructor did not touch his pupil.) Grandfather Capps wears a quasi-military jacket but the other three men wear the striped bathing-costumes with long legs and high necks that were the basic style for men in the 1890s, although these costumes are sleeveless. Most men's costumes in the 1890s had very short sleeves. Although they cannot be seen in this photograph, the Capps' bathing-machines, like those at Tenby, carried advertisements for Beecham's Pills.*

service of which many holidaymakers have fond memories. Their clothes were those fashionable for women of their own class and time. Suitable dress for a seaside landlady would have been neat, respectable and of a cut and style to inspire confidence in her guests. It would always have been one step in fashion below the clothes of the guests she hoped to attract and serve.

Servants in a high-class boarding house or a grand hotel wore the clothes of servants everywhere.

Beach vendors and services

One of the reasons why the earliest, and subsequently bigger, seaside resorts were noisy was that the beaches were seen as a free sales area by any working person with something to sell. Continuing a tradition several centuries old of 'crying' their wares, the street traders moved on to the beaches, and from the time that visitors began to sit on the beaches they were subjected to people trying to sell them something. The wares offered ranged from fish, fruit, watercress, cakes or drinks to beach toys, games equipment (including buckets and spades) or souvenirs. National acts to control street trading were passed in 1871 and 1881, and street and beach vendors were required to be licensed.

Apart from the distinctive clothes of the fisherfolk, most of these beach traders wore the ordinary clothes common to the

107. *Crying their wares. Vendors on the seaside promenade in the 1860s. A sketch by John Leech.*

108. *Two women beach vendors near the end of the day at Hastings in the 1890s,
photographed by George Woods. They are both older women wearing unfashionable
clothes, bonnets and large white aprons. Their heavy skirts are decorated with tucks at the
bottom. Their blouses or bodices are hidden. The woman on the left wears a long cape with
slits in the sides through which she puts her arms. She appears to be wearing long knitted
sleeves under a shorter full sleeve gathered in to a band below the elbow. Her empty basket
stands on the ground beside her while she chats to the other woman, who wears a fringed
shawl over her shoulders. It is not known what they sold but the shawled woman's basket
has a white cloth over it; she may have sold cakes or home-made sweets.*

general working-class people of their time, with the addition of aprons if necessary. In the 1860s these clothes included shabby trousers, waistcoats and jackets of corduroy, serge or kersey (a coarse woollen cloth) for men, with white or blue aprons. Women wore ankle-length skirts, large white, fawn or checked aprons and long shawls. Dull reddish brown was a popular colour for women's skirts. Both sexes wore hats and boots, although the woman's head wear was more usually a bonnet. This could range from a white cotton sun-bonnet to a battered 'coal scuttle' shape in black straw or bombazine. Their wares were sold from baskets on the beach, or from trestle tables set up for the purpose. On the promenade above the beach wheelbarrows and hand-carts were used.

The clothes of beach vendors changed only in their details over a forty-year period. They were always out of date as far as fashion was concerned. In the 1890s women beach traders were

109. *Tea ready on the shore — a beach refreshment hut about 1900; it is not known where the photograph was taken. The trestle tables would have been packed away into the hut at night. Fresh water would have been brought to the beach in buckets. Bottled mineral water was available at this time and was probably as popular as tea.*

110. *The beach stall at Scarborough in 1905 sold buckets and spades for children, shrimping nets, Union Jack flags and other beach toys. The proprietor and his wife are a respectably dressed young couple. He is in grey trousers and jacket with a darker peaked cap; she is in a dark skirt, fashionable white blouse and black broad-brimmed hat.*

still wearing boots, shawls and aprons, but by this time their skirts were instep length and their head wear could as easily be a hat with a brim as a bonnet. Black was now the most popular colour for beach traders' clothes, worn with a white apron. By the 1890s flowers, toffee-apples and ice-cream (sold from little barrows containing chunks of ice to keep it cool) had been added to the range of items sold on the beach and promenade. By the 1890s, too, some male beach traders dressed in fishermen's jerseys, even those whose trade had nothing to do with fish, and especially the vendors of souvenirs, which included seashells, and the sellers of beach toys, buckets and spades.

Among the promenade traders in Edwardian times were shoeblacks — offering to polish shoes as visitors left the beach — and newspaper boys. Down on the beach the traders were joined by fortune-tellers, using dogs or lovebirds to pick out cards foretelling their clients' future, and photographers. The photographers, who worked with portable dark-rooms on hand-carts, were usually more formally dressed than other beach traders, conveying an air of respectability by their clothing — light

111 (above). *The Hastings hairdresser William Dine wearing a white apron over a dark suit. His shop was a converted fisherman's netshop in Eastbeach Street, and his clients were more often the fishermen than the visitors, for he often rowed out to the fishing boats to shave the crews before they came ashore. He wore his hat even when he was at work in the shop. His companions are local residents, the woman in a plain dark dress and a white apron, the man in dark suit and small cap.*

112 (left). *A fortune-teller on Hastings beach using love-birds which picked out a ball that told clients' 'past and future life'. She wears a dark pleated skirt trimmed with a lighter band of fabric, a coloured apron, a white blouse, a brightly patterned bolero and a handkerchief folded over her hair. Her middle-aged client wears light trousers, a dark jacket with rounded lower fronts and a cloth cap with a peak.*

trousers, frock-coats or morning coats, bowler hats or soft caps.

After the First World War beach salesmen gradually disappeared. Small shops along the promenade took their place, or vendors on tricycles — also on the promenade — sold candy floss or ice-cream, while tea-houses, in small chalets in the municipal parks or on lawns or walkways above the beach, provided refreshment. Much of this change was due to the various Acts of Parliament regarding the sale of food and drink that have been passed in the twentieth century. Municipal bylaws changed: gone were the old laws about bathing-machines. Bylaws of the 1920s and 1930s took in hygiene — public conveniences were built — and excessive noise: 'crying one's wares' was strictly prohibited.

The beach attendants changed, too. The bathing women and swimming instructors of the Victorians and Edwardians gave way to the man who hired out the deck-chairs. He usually wore a linen jacket and a peaked cap and carried a bag on a shoulder-strap for the money he took.

The photographers, too, moved up to the promenade and no longer worked from portable dark-rooms. Instead they snapped away at passers-by, handing them a ticket to take later to the studio, to collect their prints. The photographs taken actually on the beach were those taken by the holidaymakers themselves,

113 (right). *This picture of one of the beach photographers at Hastings in the 1890s was taken by George Woods, whose collection of Hastings prints includes photographs of at least four different beach photographers with portable dark-rooms mounted on little hand-carts. They produced tintype portraits on the beach for the visitors. This photographer is very respectably dressed in a dark morning coat over lighter-coloured trousers. He normally wears a bowler hat, a very useful accessory as illustrated in this picture, for he may well have been about to use it to cover the lens of his camera to regulate the length of exposure of the glass negative when taking his picture.*

114. *'Stop me and buy one': the original Wall's tricycle for ice-cream sales was introduced in 1922 at Acton, London. The tricycles were not refrigerated so could not go far from their depots, but by 1939 some 8500 tricycles were based at 136 depots in the larger inland and seaside towns. The 'ice-cream men' wore dark trousers and a jacket made from a thin blue and white striped material with dark blue facings and collar. They also wore a stiff peaked cap with a metal badge.*

using a Box Brownie camera or a folding Kodak bellows camera to produce the holiday prints that exist today in millions of family albums.

The entertainers

The Victorians on seaside beaches were not only beset by salespeople with baskets of goods but were also pursued by entertainers, so that most activities had a musical accompaniment. This music included single street or beach singers, musicians playing accordions, hurdy-gurdies, fiddles or even handbells, and itinerant German bands, as well as the organised band concerts, minstrel shows and concert parties that came to be an expected part of an English seaside holiday.

Gradually the organised entertainers took over from the single singers and musicians. Military or municipal bands played in bandstands built on the promenade or the pier. The first minstrel troupe, an 'Ethiopian band' called the Virginian Minstrels, came

115. *The beach bus from Rye to Winchelsea Beach in the 1930s. The driver wears grey flannels, a linen jacket with a badge pinned on it and a white peaked cap. Apart from the cap and badge, his clothes were very little different from those that would have been worn by the holidaymakers he carried. The conductor wears a double-breasted grey suit and a white peaked cap and carries his money-bag and ticket-punch on straps over his shoulders. The tickets, coloured pieces of printed paper, are carried in a little clipboard in his hand. It is not known who the third man is, but he wears a dark suit with a waistcoat; this was almost a uniform for older working men. Even at leisure they wore the same type of clothes, occasionally substituting a grey or white linen jacket for the dark jacket of the suit. He wears a tweed flat cap. All three men wear collars and ties.*

to England from the United States in 1843 and caused a sensation, as much by their black make-up and brilliant blazers as by the plantation songs they presented. By the 1860s few of the original American minstrels remained in England, but nearly every seaside resort had its own, English, minstrels, with blackened faces and colourful clothes, singing about plantations that none of them had ever seen. But the holidaymakers enjoyed the music, and the popularity of the 'blacked-up' minstrel bands and singing troupes lasted for over fifty years, until they were ousted by the equally popular pierrots, performing on makeshift stages on the beach or in pier theatres. One of the last minstrel shows was at St Leonards-on-Sea, East Sussex, in 1900.

The first pierrot troupe was organised by a banjo player called Clifford Essex. In 1891 they played at Henley as a 'Pierrot Banjo

Band', and in 1892, now called the 'Royal Pierrots', they toured
the south coast. Their clothes were white baggy suits trimmed
with black or red pompoms. They were considered more respectable than the minstrels. At first they were all men, but as the
twentieth century progressed the pierrot troupes included
women, too, in short white skirts trimmed with pompoms.

Alongside the pierrots were the more up-market concert parties. They performed not only on the beach but also in the pier
theatres or in open-air theatres in the public gardens. Their
clothes were smarter than the pierrots'; nautical-style dress for
the men and evening gowns for the women singers were their
stage presentation clothes. Many of these performers became
famous stage and music-hall stars in the mid twentieth century
after starting in the 1920s seaside shows.

116. *The Dandy White Coons, the beach pierrots who took over from the blacked-up
minstrels at Worthing, West Sussex, in the early years of the twentieth century. Sometimes
the pierrots could afford to have a tent or bathing-hut in which to change into their costumes;
more often they arrived on the beach from their lodgings dressed in their stage costumes.
Sometimes they carried a piano on to the beach; sometimes their music was provided by
an accordion. Their stage was crude and primitive, with no wings or scenery, but many of
the famous entertainers of the mid twentieth century started at the seaside as young pierrots
or concert-party performers.*

117. *A beach concert party at Hastings in the 1890s. They have no stage and have carried a small harmonium down on to the pebbles, where it is played by a man in light trousers and a blazer. The singer wears a light-coloured suit and the third member of the concert party a dark suit. All three wear straw boaters with coloured ribbons. Concert party artistes were considered a cut above the blacked-up minstrels and the pierrots that followed them; they wore fairly smart but conventional leisure clothes.*

118. *The old 'Minstrel Ring' at Great Yarmouth, during or just before the First World War. This area of the upper beach was first fenced off in 1897 and a stage erected for minstrel shows. From about 1900 it was used by a number of concert parties. This photograph shows a performance by members of Chappell's concert party. The two girl singers are wearing large straw hats, sailor blouses, short striped skirts and black stockings. They are probably singing a patriotic song and their costumes might well be red, white and blue.*

119 (left). *Miss Minnie Johnson, the teenage demonstration swimmer at Brighton. In 1890 she swam from the Chain Pier to the West Pier in 36 minutes 25 seconds wearing a theatrical-style bathing-dress.*

120 (right). *The Punch and Judy show at Morecambe in 1928. The puppets and the booths have changed little since the mid nineteenth century. The twentieth-century children watching wear short dresses and woollen cardigans. Some wear knitted or crocheted little bonnets or berets; two older girls wear cloche hats. The little boys wear shorts and shirts or jerseys. Some boys are wearing school blazers and small caps, others the larger baker-boy caps.*

As well as concert-party performances there were other entertainers on the piers. There were the aquatic performers who gave exhibitions of diving or swimming either off the end of the pier, in the water around the pier or even in tanks of water on the piers. Many of the male high-divers in their knee-length costumes called themselves 'Professor' — 'Professor' Pouncey at Southport and 'Professor' Reddish at Brighton — while the female swimmers were always genteel young ladies. In 1890 Miss Minnie Johnson gave daily swimming performances in a tank on Brighton Pier, in the course of which she would drink a glass of lemonade and eat a slice of cake while completely submerged. She was still giving this performance on music-hall stages nearly forty years later in the late 1920s, supplementing her income by teaching swimming to young children for 2s 6d for a course of six lessons. These lessons were in the sea, and even in the summer of 1927 Miss Johnson still wore a Victorian bathing-dress consisting

121. *A drawing by John Leech, c.1860, showing two Victorian evangelists holding a service on the beach. They are formally dressed, one in a black frock-coat, the other in a cutaway coat, and have tall top-hats. The holidaymakers are dressed informally, although they all wear hats and even the little girl wears a hooped crinoline.*

122. *Members of a seaside mission team from the Methodist Cliff College, Sheffield, in 1937. The groups of students who took part in beach missions led services on beaches all round England. In the 1930s they were very popular in the north of England. Their clothes were comparable to those worn by many of the holidaymakers; they used songs, accordion music and good humour to convey their message.*

of black stockings and bloomers under a deep-bodiced top with a short skirt and full, frilled, short sleeves.

Other seaside entertainers were the brass bandsmen, performing on municipal bandstands on the promenade, in public gardens or on the piers. These band performances date back to the 1870s. While some genuine military bands played at the seaside, in full regulation band uniform, other, civilian bands usually wore military-style uniforms. At the same time orchestras were equally popular, and at Worthing a ladies' string orchestra, dressed all in black, performed at the end of the pier in the early 1890s.

On the beach the Punch and Judy puppet booths were always popular with children. Photographs taken as far apart as 1880 and 1930 show rapt children watching almost identical booths and puppets. Only the children's clothes changed as the years went by.

As early as the 1860s, and possibly earlier, beach evangelists were holding open-air services on the beaches on Sundays. They were of all denominations. At first they were highly noticeable because of their formal clothes which contrasted with the more casual clothes of the holidaymakers, but by the 1930s they wore equally casual clothes and offered entertainment based on Bible stories in open-air Sunday schools for children on holiday.

123. The changing image. In the late 1930s the Mayor of St Leonards-on-Sea opened the miniature railway on the beach by driving the first train. It was obviously not a hot sunny day for the children in the train wear cardigans or blazers over summer dresses or shorts. Many of the adults watching are wearing mackintoshes. In all the crowd there are only two older men, the policeman, one woman and one very small child wearing hats.

8. Tailpiece: the preparation for war

In the summer of 1939 there was a change to the British seaside resorts. While it was business as usual for those on the north-west and Welsh coasts, along the south and east coasts preparations had begun for war. Many people hoped it would not come, but on 4th September 1939 war was declared between Britain and Germany. During the winter of 1939-40 the clothes worn on the beaches of southern and eastern England were those of the Army or civil defence units who erected concrete and iron blocks along the top of the beaches, laid miles of coiled barbed-wire at the tide mark, buried mines in the shingle and built a network of inter-leaved iron poles on the part of the beaches exposed at low tide in the hope that all this would help deter the invasion of England by German forces.

124. *Men of the 1st/4th Essex Regiment wiring defences at Embleton Bay, on the Northumberland coast, in 1940. The east coast of England was fortified before the south, for before the fall of France the threatened invasion route was through Holland.*

9. Further reading

As far as the author can discover there are no books devoted to the study of clothes worn at the seaside, other than this one. Many costume books, however, mention bathing-costumes as part of a general text, as do several books about the growth and history of the seaside. The libraries or museums in many seaside resorts have published books on their own towns or on local photographers, and these have included photographs of people on the beach. This bibliography features a selection of such books, all of which mention clothes worn at the seaside. There are many other similar books.

Costume history
Colmer, M. *Bathing Beauties; the Amazing History of Female Swimwear.* Sphere Books, 1977.
Cunnington, C. Willet and Phillis. *English Costume in the Nineteenth Century.* Faber and Faber, 1966.
Cunnington, C. Willet and Phillis. *English Costume in the Twentieth Century.* Faber and Faber, 1967.
Tozer, Jane, and Levitt, Sarah. *Fabric of Society 1770-1870.* Laura Ashley, 1983.

Seaside history
Anderson, Janet, and Swinglehurst, Edmund. *The Victorian and Edwardian Seaside.* Country Life, 1978.
Bainbridge, Cyril. *Pavilions on the Sea.* Robert Hale, 1968. A history of the seaside pleasure pier.
Bridgeman, H. *Beside the Seaside.* Elm Tree Books, 1977. A picture postcard album.
Marsdon, Christopher. *The English at the Seaside.* Collins, 1948.
Walvin, James. *Beside the Seaside.* Allen Lane, 1978. A social history.

Local history
Haworth-Booth, Mark. *A Yarmouth Holiday.* Dirk Nishen Publishing, 1988. Photographs by Paul Martin.
Rhoden, Irene, and Peak, George. *George Woods.* Midnight Press, Hastings, 1987. Hastings photographs of the 1890s.
Worsley, Roger. *Prince of Places.* Laidlow Burgess, c.1976. Photographs of Tenby by Charles Smith-Allen.

For children

Goodall, John S. *An Edwardian Holiday*. Macmillan, 1978. A picture book without text.

125. *A bathing-dress of 1902 from the collection in Worthing Museum. It is made of red and white striped cotton twill, now very faded, trimmed with red and white braid. The red collar is edged with white braid and has an appliquéd white anchor motif. The label inside is inscribed 'Patent 12212 W. British Make'.*

10. Places to visit

Seaside museums with costume collections will probably have an example of a swimming costume or bathing-dress. However, these costumes may not be on permanent exhibition and the serious student should enquire before visiting. Clothes in the museum's store can usually be seen by appointment. There are several important inland costume collections in the British Isles which have bathing or beach clothes in their collections and arrangements for these to be seen can also be made by appointment. The museums listed here all have bathing clothes in their collections.

Bexhill Manor Museum of Costume and Social History, Manor House Gardens, Old Town, Bexhill, East Sussex TN40 2AP. Telephone: 0424 215361.

Brighton Art Gallery and Museum, Church Street, Brighton, East Sussex BN1 1UE. Telephone: 0273 603005.

Castle Howard Costume Galleries, Castle Howard, York, North Yorkshire YO6 7DA. Telephone: 065384 333 extension 34.

Gallery of English Costume, Platt Hall, Rusholme, Manchester M14 5LL. Telephone: 061-224 5217.

The Hollytrees Museum, High Street, Colchester, Essex CO1 1UG. Telephone: 0206 712493.

Liverpool Museum, William Brown Street, Liverpool, Merseyside L3 8EN. Telephone: 051-207 0001 or 5451.

Museum of Costume, Bennett Street, Bath, Avon BA1 2QH. Telephone: 0225 461111.

Rougemont House Museum of Costume and Lace, Castle Street, Exeter, Devon. Telephone: 0392 265858.

Victoria and Albert Museum, Cromwell Road, South Kensington, London SW7 2RL. Telephone: 071-938 8500.

Welholme Galleries, Welholme Road, Grimsby, South Humberside DN32 9LP. Telephone: 0472 242000 extension 1385.

Welsh Folk Museum, St Fagans, Cardiff, South Glamorgan CF5 6XB. Telephone: 0222 569441.

Wordspring Museum, Burlington Street, Weston-super-Mare, Avon BS23 1PR. Telephone: 0934 621028.

Worthing Museum and Art Gallery, Chapel Road, Worthing, West Sussex BN11 1HD. Telephone: 0903 39999 extension 121.

Acknowledgements

A book like this cannot be written without the help of a great many people. The author is grateful to her husband, Howard Lansdell, and to Sidney Renow for copying and printing photographs for research, many of which are included in this book; to Marion van der Voort and Kay Corben for typing text and captions; to Doreen Carey for the loan of her collection of fashion prints; and to the many other people who loaned their family albums or collections and answered innumerable questions. These included Julian Dunn, James Fenton, Vivienne McKenzie, Mary Midgeley, Colin Osman and Sidney Renow, as well as Pamela Haines of the Hastings Central Library, Catherine Clinton of the Yarmouth Central Library, Anthea Jarvis of the Gallery of English Costume, Platt Hall, Manchester, the staffs of the Hastings Museum, the Tenby Museum, the Worthing Museum, the Yarmouth Museum and the Royal Archives. There were many others, too, who gave time and knowledge to help the book along.

The pictures are acknowledged as follows: by gracious permission of Her Majesty the Queen, 45, 57; Jackie Allen, 21; Bette Anderson, title page, 72, 91; Bexhill Museum, 105; Birdseye Walls, 114; Doreen Carey, 1, 10, 18, 29, 31; the late Philip Daniell, 6, 7, 77, 88, 99; the Reverend Vere Ducker, 50; Julian Dunn, 49, 51, 63, 78; East Sussex County Library, Hastings Library, 38, 108; James Fenton, 28, 42, 109, 110, 120; the late Arthur Gill, 97; Hastings Museum, 8, 35, 36, 37, 39, 40, 41, 75, 98, 101, 111, 112, 113, 123; the Hulton Picture Library, 76; the Imperial War Museum, 124; Chris Latford, 34, 43; the Gallery of English Costume, Manchester City Art Galleries, 13, 16, 17; Vivienne McKenzie, 67, 74, 84; Mary Midgeley, 58, 86; John Moorley, 122; National Museum of Photography, Film and Television, page 2; Colin Osman, 12, 23, 26, 70; L. S. Parker, 95; John Pulford, 115; Sidney Renow, 56, 89; Richmond Museum, page 3, 82; Tom Salt, 66, 80; George Stift, 119; Tenby Museum, 102, 104; Victoria and Albert Museum, 32, 53; Weybridge Museum, cover, 9, 14, 15, 52, 54, 55, 62, 68, 69, 81, 85, 93, 94, 100, 107, 121; Worthing Museum, 2, 90, 116; Yarmouth Library, 65, 118; Great Yarmouth Museum (Norfolk Museums Service), 106. All other pictures are from the author's collection.

Index
Page numbers in italic refer to illustrations.